# THE KIDS' SUMMER HANDBOOK

# THE KIDS' SUMMER HANDBOOK

BY JANE DRAKE & ANN LOVE

ILLUSTRATED BY HEATHER COLLINS

TICKNOR & FIELDS / BOOKS FOR YOUNG READERS

NEW YORK · 1994

First American edition 1994 published by
Ticknor & Fields / Books for Young Readers
A Houghton Mifflin company, 215 Park Avenue South, New
York, New York 10003.

First published in Canada as *The Kids Cottage Book,* by Kids
Can Press Ltd.

Many designations used by manufacturers and sellers to
distinguish their products are claimed as trademarks. Where
those designations appear in this book and Ticknor & Fields
Books for Young Readers was aware of a trademark claim, the
designations have been printed in intitial capital letters (i.e.,
Popsicle).

Neither the publisher nor the author nor the illustrator shall be
liable for any damage which may be caused or sustained as a
result of the conduct of any of the activities in this book, from not
specifically following instructions or conducting the activities
without proper supervision, or from ignoring the cautions
contained in the text

Manufactured in the United States of America

Book design by Blair Kerrigan/Glyphics
The text of this book is set in 12 pt. New Century Schoolbook.

BP  10  9  8  7  6  5

*Library of Congress Cataloging-in-Publication Data*
Drake, Jane.
The Kids' Summer Handbook / by Jane Drake & Ann Love ;
illustrated by Heather Collins.
p. cm.
Includes index.
ISBN 0-395-68711-X (cl) — ISBN 0-395-68709-8 (pa)
1. Outdoor recreation for children—Juvenile literature. 2.
Handicraft—Juvenile literature. 3. Nature craft—Juvenile
literature.
[1. Nature craft. 2. Handicraft. 3. Outdoor recreation.]
I. Love, Ann. II. Collins, Heather, ill. III. Title.
GV191.62.D73 1994
790.1'22—dc20
93-2524     CIP     AC

*This book is dedicated to*

**Jim, Stephanie, Brian, Madeline**
**&**
**David, Melanie, Jennifer, Adrian**

*with whom we have loved and savored*
*many happy, crazy, and active*
*summer days.*
*We're looking forward to*
*many more to come.*

# CONTENTS

# ACKNOWLEDGMENTS

The authors acknowledge the contribution to this book of the following people:
Andrea, Brianna, Natalie, and Hilary Barnett and their family at Shuswap Lake; Greg and Patrick Barnett and their parents; Kathleen and Henry Barnett and every kid who loves Pipsissewoods; Donna Bennett; Cathi Bremner; Jack Brickenden; Jessica Bartram and her parents; Saran Bickram; Nellie Chisholm; Kathy and Bob Clay; Jane Crist; Kurt Crist; Mary Dobson; Chris and Mike Drake; Mary Beth Drake; Ruth and Charlie Drake and all their grandchildren at Lion's Head; Irmgardt Duley; Jane Falconi; Alan Foster; Jennie Gruss; Sara Irwin; Donald and Kathleen Leitch; Geoff and Ben Lewis and their parents; Matthew Litvak; Betty and Gage Love and all the warm fun at Westwinds and Windgage; Melanie Manchee and her whole clan; Carolyn Marshall; Kim, Brett, Janine, and Sean Passi; Mary Jean Potter; Steve and Maria Price; Hilary Robinson; Ian Sedgwick who loved the cold water of Georgian Bay; Yvonne and Jack Sellars; Stephanie Smith; Dennis Stitt; Malcolm Sweeny and his Muskoka roots; Mary and Ron Tasker; Andrew, Mary, and Doug Thompson; Douglas Wright; and Val Wyatt.

We couldn't have written this book without old and warm summer memories of Jim Baillie, Barb and Vic Barnett, Doreen Barnett, Sadie and Thomas Barnett, Bill and Peggy Clarke, Muriel Flavelle, Tony and Mary Franks, Millie and Thomas Gourlay, Kit and Murray MacDonald, Ed and Marg McClure, all the Morgans, Anne and Bron Robinson, the Spitlers, Anne and Duncan Smith, Bob and Kay Taylor, and Madeline Woolatt.

Thank you to Valerie Hussey, Ricky Englander, and all the people at Kids Can Press. It's been a great pleasure working with illustrator Heather Collins and book designer Blair Kerrigan. A special thank-you to editor Laurie Wark, a fellow cottager. She enthusiastically welcomed all ideas—traditional and unconventional—and helped us fit as much as possible into 208 pages! Thanks, too, to Norma Jean Sawicki, Robin Schneider, and Julie Amper for the U.S. edition.

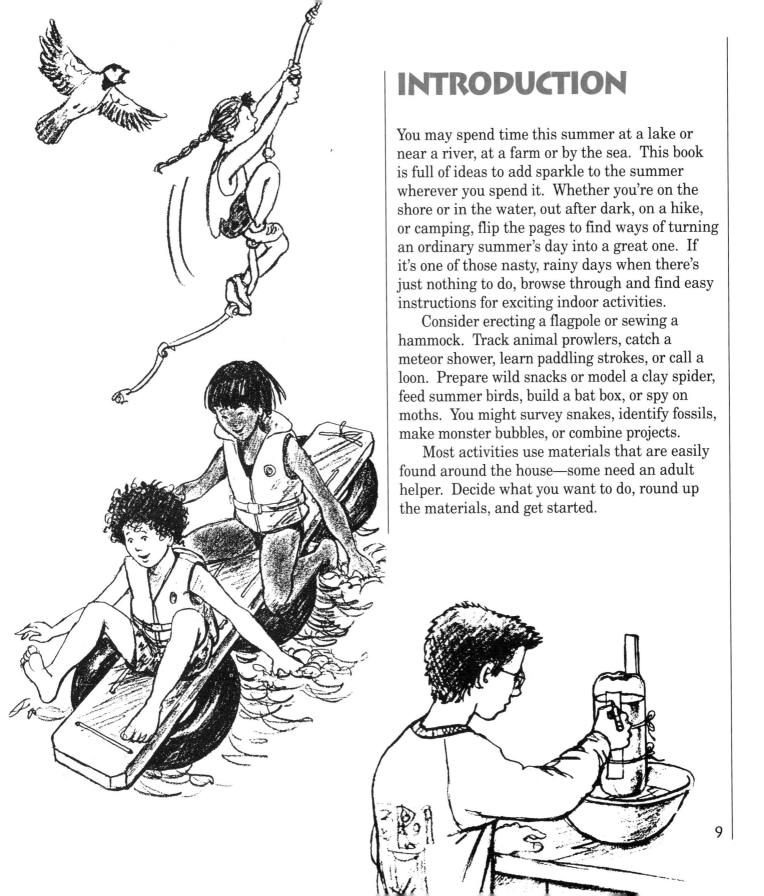

# INTRODUCTION

You may spend time this summer at a lake or near a river, at a farm or by the sea. This book is full of ideas to add sparkle to the summer wherever you spend it. Whether you're on the shore or in the water, out after dark, on a hike, or camping, flip the pages to find ways of turning an ordinary summer's day into a great one. If it's one of those nasty, rainy days when there's just nothing to do, browse through and find easy instructions for exciting indoor activities.

Consider erecting a flagpole or sewing a hammock. Track animal prowlers, catch a meteor shower, learn paddling strokes, or call a loon. Prepare wild snacks or model a clay spider, feed summer birds, build a bat box, or spy on moths. You might survey snakes, identify fossils, make monster bubbles, or combine projects.

Most activities use materials that are easily found around the house—some need an adult helper. Decide what you want to do, round up the materials, and get started.

# SHORESIDE

Head down to the shore, where land and water meet. Here's the place to make sand castles or sculptures, launch toy boats, check out creatures in the shallows, or practice water tricks. When you get too hot and need to cool off in the water, try out a swimming game. Or make a snorkel, practice the J-stroke in a canoe, or dive off a homemade raft.

# BEACH SCULPTING

**T**his may be the summer to build the biggest and most elaborate sand castle ever. The Guinness World Book record for the tallest sand castle is nineteen feet six inches high. Here are some ideas to get started on an unbeatable castle creation.

## PREPARING FOR THE CASTLE CHALLENGE

Get ready to build a gigantic sand castle by gathering many different sizes of plastic containers. Look for empty yogurt cups, margarine containers, flowerpots, even a toothpaste cap. Dessert molds, cookie cutters, pot lids and springform pans will make unusual shapes. (Check with an adult before taking kitchen items to the beach.) An empty plastic soda bottle with the top cut off becomes a pail with a fancy design on the bottom. Empty clam shells can be used as well. For massive undertakings, a shovel or other garden tools may be necessary. You'll also need a Popsicle stick or a smooth piece of driftwood to round out the contours of the castle.

The best sand castles are made with moist but not sloppy sand. Fill the containers with sand and pack them well before turning them upside down and unmolding. If the sand sticks to the container, squeeze the top of it to loosen.

## GOING FOR THE GUINNESS RECORD

**1.**
Start with the largest container and make the foundations and walls. Then use the smaller containers to add character to the creation. Fill the soda bottle with wet sand to create turrets.

**2.**
Finishing touches can be added with pinecones, feathers, sticks, shells, stones, and driftwood.

**3.**
If you're with a friend, work together to make an entire town. Be sure to collect all of the containers and tools when finished building.

# SCULPTURES

Sand sculptures are easy to make using your hands and a shovel. Firmly pack moist sand with your hands. Use your imagination to decide what to sculpt in the sand, but here are a few suggestions to get started.

## SAND MONSTERS

Frighten people away with Everglades creatures. Snakes, alligators, crabs, and a crouching panther will make a swampy scene. Add a tangle of sticks and twigs with some greenery to create a mangrove habitat.

## SCHOOLS OF BEACH FISH

Go fishing without the rod and reel. Make an entire school of fish that appear to swim through the sand, with pebble scales that catch the sun.

# DRIBBLE CASTLES

Sit at the edge of the water where the sand is wet—just beyond the reach of the waves. Take a large handful or pailful of wet sand. Let it slowly dribble into a pile, moving your hand in a circular motion to create a lumpy, swirly structure. It won't look like a conventional castle, but it will look striking when it dries. Keep the sand very wet while working with it.

## SAND DINOSAURS

Recreate the Mesozoic era (the age of the dinosaurs) complete with prehistoric creatures by sculpting *Stegosaurus*, *Tyrannosaurus rex*, or *Brontosaurus*. Use twigs and driftwood to complete the landscape.

## FEEDING THE GULLS

Befriend the local gull flock with stale bread and leftover toast. Collect a plate of bread scraps after each meal. At the end of each day, go down to the water's edge and call, "Here gully, gully, gully." Wait for the first gull to fly by and toss it a small morsel. Within seconds every gull around will be sweeping overhead. Try to throw the bread high enough so the gulls will catch it in the air.

   Begin every feeding session with the call "Here gully, gully, gully." The gulls will quickly learn to recognize your voice and associate it with dinnertime!

# BEACH MAGIC

**H**ere are some tricks to do by the water to amaze yourself and your friends.

## WATER STANDING UPSIDE DOWN

If you turn a pail of water upside down, the water will pour out, right? Fill a small beach pail with water about halfway. Swing it back and forth to build up speed. Then, with your arm straight, swing it fast in circles, from your knees right up and over your head. Even when the pail is upside down at the top, the water will stay in it. Why? As long as the water is moving quickly along a circular path, centrifugal force holds it in place. If you stop swinging the pail and hold it still over head, watch out!

## UPHILL CLIMBING WATER

Water never flows uphill, right? Dip one end of a dry beach towel in the water and stretch the other end up and over a rock or shrub out of the water. Come back in an hour and see how far water has crept uphill. Water is made up of tiny particles called molecules that hold onto one another and seep up the empty air spaces left in the weave of the towel. This is called capillary action and is the reason a towel dries you off.

# TYING WATER IN KNOTS

Try this trick to bend water and tie it together with your fingers.

With a nail, prick five small holes of equal size in a line near the bottom of a plastic container. The holes should be about a quarter-inch apart. Fill the pail with water and set it on a flat surface. Five spouts of water should be coming out. Gently pinch the five spouts together with your finger and thumb. Release quickly so your fingers don't brush against the knot made in the water. Why does the water knot? The surface of water forms a strong and elasticlike skin where it meets the air. This property of water is called surface tension. In this trick, you shape the skin slightly.

Some water insects have hairy feet that act like snowshoes, spreading the insects' weight out over the surface of the water so they can walk on the skin of the water.

## DEAD CALM

Moving water pushes harder than still water—or does it?

Fill a plastic spray bottle with water—an empty dishwashing-soap squirt bottle will do. Line up two toy boats on still water so they float beside each other. Now spray hard on the water between them. Instead of pushing them apart, the spraying water drives the boats together. The still water on the outside of the boats has greater pressure than the moving water between them. The greater power of the calm water pushes the boats together and causes a crash.

15

# SAND CRAFTS

## SAND CANDLES

These candles are made right on the beach. The sand sticks to the outside of the wax, giving the candle an interesting, scratchy surface. They're perfect for the dining room table or as summer birthday gifts.

**You'll need:**

| |
|---|
| a small garden or beach shovel and a ruler |
| a 10-inch piece of string |
| a short stick |
| a small ball of modeling clay |
| old crayons or candle stubs |
| a clean, empty coffee can |
| an old double boiler or heavy pot |
| tap water |
| a stove (and an adult helper) |
| pot holders |

**1.**
Dig a hole in the sand about four inches wide and eight inches deep.

**2.**
Tie one end of the string to the middle of the stick. Attach the clay ball to the other end of the string.

**3.**
Ask an adult to help melt the crayons or candles. Fill the large can halfway with candle and crayon stubs. Place the can in the pot.

**4.**
Fill the pot halfway with warm water.

**5.**
Place the pot on the stove. Turn on low heat. The wax will take about twenty minutes to melt. As the wax melts, add more crayons and candles. The melted wax should never fill more than half the can. If you're making a big candle, it's better to melt the wax in two batches.

**6.**
Using the pot holders, remove the can from the pot and carry it down to the beach.

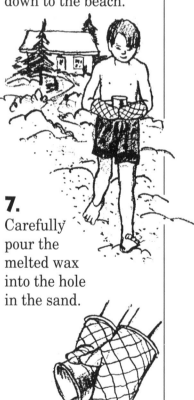

**7.**
Carefully pour the melted wax into the hole in the sand.

**8.**

Lower the string into the middle of the wax, with the clay ball in the wax and the stick lying across the top of the hole to hold the string straight through the wax.

**9.**

Allow the wax to cool and harden for at least eight hours. Surround the candle with rocks or sticks so people won't step in it.

**10.**

Use the shovel to ease any sand away from the top rim of the hardened candle. Slowly lift the candle out of the hole. Brush off excess sand with your hands.

# SAND GOOP

If you ever wanted to take a sand castle home, here's how to make a permanent sand castle.

| You'll need: |
| --- |
| 2 cups sand |
| 1 cup cornstarch |
| 1 tbsp powdered alum (available at a drugstore) |
| $3/4$ cup water |
| an old pot |
| a stove |
| a wooden spoon |
| newspaper |
| sandpaper |
| acrylic or poster paints |
| paintbrush |
| white glue |
| an adult helper |

**1.**

Mix the sand, cornstarch, alum, and water in the pot.

**2.**

Ask an adult to help cook the mixture over low heat, stirring constantly.

**3.**

Remove it from heat when it is thick like Play-Doh. Allow it to cool before using.

**4.**

Sand goop can be used like any modeling material. Create sand castles, sculptures, paperweights, or doorstops. As the name *goop* suggests, it is messy, so work outside or spread newspaper on a table indoors.

**5.**

Place the completed work on newspaper and allow it to dry at room temperature for several days.

**6.**

Buff it with sandpaper to remove loose sand.

**7.**

Paint the sculpture or leave it plain. Acrylic or poster paints work well.

**8.**

Painted sculptures can be sealed by brushing them with white glue.

**9.**

Any leftover sand goop can be stored for a few days in a tightly sealed container.

# HOT AND THIRSTY

**F**or those hot and sticky days of summer, here are some cool treats to quench a thirst.

## LEMON SODA

| You'll need: |
|---|
| juice of one lemon or orange |
| glass of water |
| 1 tsp sugar |
| 1 tsp baking soda |

**1.**
Mix the freshly squeezed juice with water and sugar in a glass.

**2.**
Add two ice cubes and the baking soda.

**3.**
Stir until bubbly and drink up.

## ICE POPS

When the corner store is not around the corner, make Popsicles at home.

| You'll need: |
|---|
| an ice-cube tray |
| fruit juice |
| toothpicks or Popsicle sticks broken in half |

**1.**
Fill the ice-cube tray with a favorite fruit juice.

**2.**
Stick the fat end of a toothpick into each cube. If using a broken Popsicle stick, put the smooth end of the stick in the juice.

**3.**
Place the tray in the freezer for three or four hours.

**4.**
Let the cubes stand at room temperature for a minute before removing them from the tray. Don't pull too hard on the toothpick—it may come out without the frozen fruit juice.

# SLUSHIES

Slushies are messy and sticky and perfect for hot days.

| You'll need: |
| --- |
| a spoon |
| a small clean tin can |
| 1 cup fruit juice |

**1.**
Place the spoon in the can.

**2.**
Fill the can with a favorite juice and place it in the freezer for about two hours.

**3.**
When the juice is almost frozen, stir it with the spoon and return it to the freezer for half an hour.

**4.**
Eat the slushie with the spoon, right from the can.

Try freezing seedless grapes, raspberries, or strawberries. When you're hot, thirsty, or hungry, pop them into your mouth for a cool treat.

## HOT BUGS

Listen to cicadas, or heat bugs, which make a loud noise by rubbing together two plates on their abdomens. These insects celebrate the heat when the temperature rises above 80°F.

# CARDBOARD BOATS

**C**anoes are a traditional American way to travel. They can be made from birchbark, aluminum, fiberglass, or wood, and range in size from six-foot one-seaters to sixty-foot war canoes holding eighteen people or more.

Here's how to make a waterproof cardboard canoe. The straw action figures described on page 190 will sit nicely on the seat, but don't expect them to do any paddling.

| You'll need: |
| --- |
| a 6-by-12-inch piece of stiff cardboard |
| a pencil |
| scissors |
| felt-tip markers |
| a darning needle |
| an 18-inch piece of fine, strong string |
| newspaper |
| a pot |
| a large tin can |
| paraffin wax or old candles to fill the tin can halfway |
| a stove |
| pot holders |
| tongs |
| a ruler |
| an adult helper |

**1.**
Fold the cardboard in half, lengthwise. Draw a side view of a canoe with the bottom of the canoe along the fold.

**2.**
Cut out the canoe but don't cut along the fold. Reserve two pieces of cardboard for seats.

**3.**
Use felt-tip markers to decorate the canoe.

20

**4.**

Thread the darning needle with the string. Double the string and knot it. Sew the bow and stern of the canoe as shown, using a blanket stitch. (See page 205 for blanket stitch instructions.)

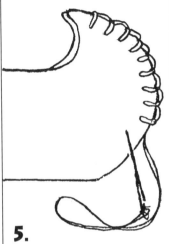

**5.**

Trim and fold the cardboard seats to fit in the hull of the canoe. Wedge in the seats snugly, as shown.

**6.**

Spread newspaper on a table or kitchen counter, and ask an adult to help with the next steps.

**7.**

Fill the cooking pot with about two inches of water. Put the wax in the can and place it in the pot.

**8.**

Heat the pot on low until the wax melts. When all the wax is melted, remove the pot from the heat. Using pot holders, take the can out of the pot and place it on the newspaper.

**9.**

Holding the cardboard canoe with the tongs, gently dip each end of the canoe into the wax.

The wax will harden very quickly. You may have to tip the can to completely cover the canoe. Allow the wax to dry for ten minutes.

Now the canoe is waterproof. Float it in shallow water or in the bathtub. Make a fleet of canoes and have a flotilla. Make a sail and race the canoe. Just slide two toothpicks between each side of the seat and tape a small square of cloth between them. Catch the breeze and it's smooth sailing!

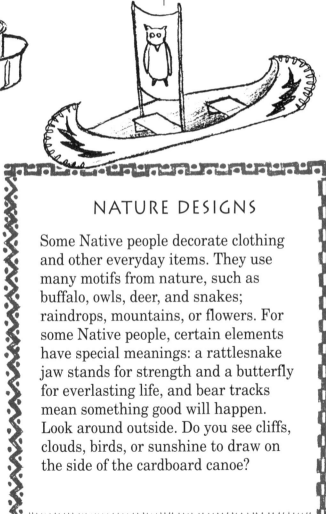

## NATURE DESIGNS

Some Native people decorate clothing and other everyday items. They use many motifs from nature, such as buffalo, owls, deer, and snakes; raindrops, mountains, or flowers. For some Native people, certain elements have special meanings: a rattlesnake jaw stands for strength and a butterfly for everlasting life, and bear tracks mean something good will happen. Look around outside. Do you see cliffs, clouds, birds, or sunshine to draw on the side of the cardboard canoe?

# BALLOON- POWERED BOAT

Here's another simple boat to make. This one is propelled with a hot-air balloon. You provide the hot air.

**You'll need:**

scissors

a milk carton

a straw that bends

heavy-duty tape

a long balloon

a nail

**1.**
Cut one side from the carton to make the boat. The pouring spout of the milk carton forms the bow.

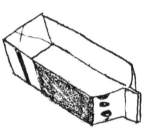

**2.**
Trim the straw so the part that bends is exactly in the middle. The straight pieces should each be about two inches long.

**3.**
Tape one end of the straw inside the balloon. Secure the tape tightly but don't collapse the straw.

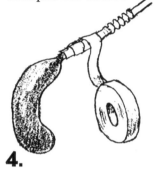

**4.**
Using the nail, poke a hole in the bottom of the carton (the stern).

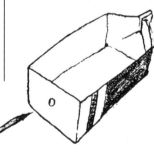

**5.**
Insert the balloon-straw "propeller" through the hole in the stern. Pull the straw through and bend it up at a ninety-degree angle.

**6.**
Blow up the balloon. Then hold the end of the straw with one finger.

**7.**
Now launch the balloon boat in water by letting go of the straw.

Race two boats and see which one runs out of hot air first.

# BALSAM RACERS

Balsam fir is an evergreen tree that grows near lake shores. It has small needles that are green on top and white underneath, growing on twigs in flat sprays. The bark is smooth with bubblelike blisters. In pioneer days, people made chewing gum with balsam resin. If there are balsam fir trees nearby, make balsam racers.

**1.**
Poke a small stick into a blister on the balsam trunk. A gum called resin will ooze out. All you need is a small blob of resin.

**2.**
Lay the stick on the surface of the water with the resin-coated end nearest the shore. The stick will shoot forward, leaving a slick in its wake. The racer moves like this because the oil in the resin, which is light and floats, spreads over the surface skin of the water, propelling the stick forward. (For more information on surface tension, see page 15.)

**3.**
Launch several balsam racers together to see which goes the farthest and the fastest before they "run out of gas."

E C O WATCH
## LAST CALL FOR THE LOON

The laughter of loons is a rarity these days. In recent years, people have been making life nearly impossible for loons. These beautiful diving birds have had deformed offspring because they fed on poisoned fish; they have starved because acid rain has killed off their prey; and now their water-level nests are being swamped by the wakes of speeding power boats. If you are lucky enough to have loons living nearby, help protect them. Drive boats well away from shore. Make "No Wake, Nesting Birds" signs to warn other boaters. Help keep the loons' call from disappearing. (To learn to cry like a loon, see page 75.)

# CRAYFISH TRAP

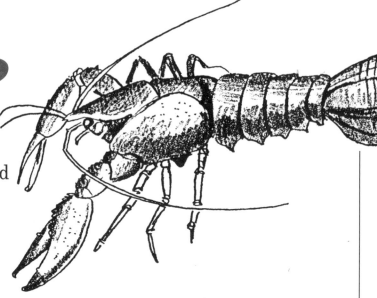

**A** flash of silver darts underwater. It may be a crayfish waving its claws and checking out your toes. Take a step—and the crayfish vanishes into the rocks.

Here's how to make a crayfish trap so that you can get a good look at one.

| You'll need: |
| --- |
| 2 one-quart plastic net berry boxes |
| 4 twist ties |
| a pocket knife |
| a thin, bending willow branch and a ruler |
| a piece of hot dog |

**1.**
Hold the two berry boxes so the openings touch and then bind them together all the way around with the twist ties. This is now a closed trap.

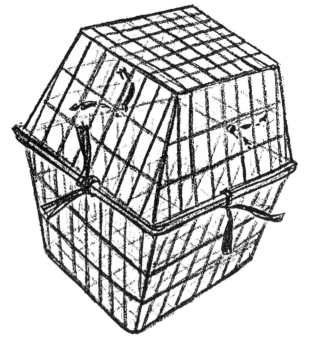

**2.**
At one end of the trap, slit the plastic net along the bottom edge and partway up two sides to make a flap. Bend the flap into the trap.

**3.**
Carefully slice the branch into four 2 ½-inch lengths and sharpen one end of each. Always stroke away from the body. (See Knife Safety on page 117.)

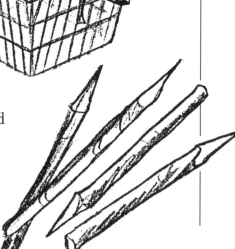

**4.**

Turn the trap so the cut box is on the bottom and the flap opens from the side into the trap. Poke one willow length through the top left corner of the flap and one through the top right corner, pointed ends first. Weave them through the mesh down each side of the flap and out the trap bottom, leaving a small opening in the bottom.

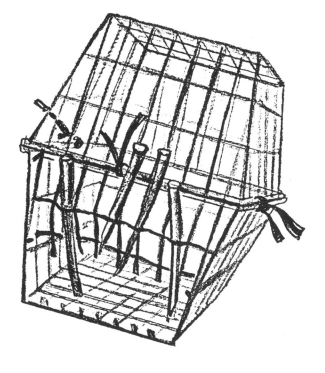

**5.**

Weave two more lengths down the middle of the flap. Stop just before the tips reach the flap bottom.

**6.**

Push a slice of hotdog into the trap.

**7.**

Put the trap underwater near rocks where you've seen crayfish and leave it overnight. Anchor the trap with a string tied to a stone.

**8.**

Check the trap in the morning. If you've caught a crayfish, take a good look. Then let it go by pushing the flap in and washing the creature out.

## SECOND NATURE

Many people around the world eat crayfish. Crayfish are related to shrimp, lobster, and crab. Northern varieties are too small for humans to want to eat but just the right size for a fish like the large-mouthed bass. If a hungry bass snaps at a crayfish and bites off only one claw, the crayfish will simply grow another claw.

**9.**

Store the trap out of the water so it doesn't accidentally catch something.

25

# SWAMP THINGS

**I**n the swamp there is an insect that will pierce the skin of a victim three times its size, turn all the victim's insides into a soup, and suck them out. Water tigers are just one of many minibeasts that live in swamp water. Here's how to take a closer look at some of these bugs and plants.

| You'll need: |
| --- |
| a medium-size pail |
| a small plastic container (such as a margarine or yogurt container) |
| a large glass bottle (such as a huge pickle jar) |
| a white sheet or countertop |

**1.**
Carry the pail and plastic container to the nearest still-water pond or swamp. Wear rubber boots and take along a friend.

**2.**
Stand on a firm spot at the edge of the swamp and dip the plastic container into the water. When you catch a "swamp thing," pour it into the pail. If the water is muddy, let it settle before pouring the cleared water into the pail.

**3.**
Fill the pail with only as much as you can carry.

**4.**
Pour the swamp water into the jar and put it on a white sheet or countertop away from direct sunlight. Do not cover the jar. (If there is leftover swamp water in the pail, return it to the swamp.)

**5.**
Take a look every day at the jar. Creatures will drastically change or fall prey to hungry predators. Some will lay eggs you cannot see and then the adults will disappear. New life will suddenly appear when the tiny eggs in the rich swamp water hatch. These are the daily dramas of the swamp.

**6.**
Add a little fresh swamp water every morning so the creatures will always have a food supply.

**7.**
After watching the swamp things for a few days, return the creatures and their water to their home. Lower the pail into the swamp and pour out the water slowly.

**SAFETY ALERT**
Do not collect swamp things where there may be danger from wild animals, such as poisonous snakes or alligators.

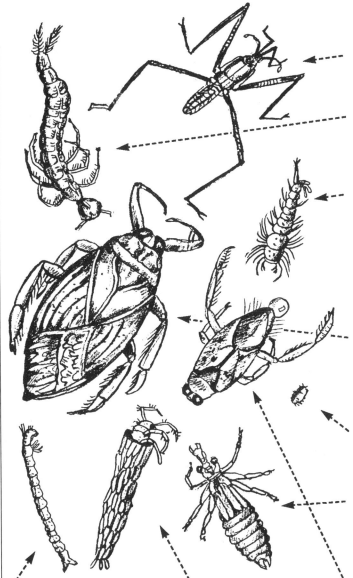

**The water strider** lives on the surface of the swamp and never sinks.

The **water tiger** injects its prey with a juice that digests the victim's body before it's eaten.

**The mosquito larva** uses a breathing tube like a snorkel it sticks through the surface of the water. Watch for a mosquito to hatch out of the water, dry its wings, and fly away.

The female **giant water bug** cements her eggs onto the back of the male, which carries them until they hatch.

That tiny red dot with eight whirling legs is probably a **water mite**.

A **dragonfly nymph** jerks along the bottom because it moves by squirting water out of its behind.

If you see two black eyes on a see-through body, this creature is probably a **phantom midge larva**. You can see it best by holding a piece of black paper behind the jar. Like all ghosts, the phantom midge larva is most active at night.

A bunch of twigs swimming together is probably the house of a **caddisfly larva**. Look carefully and a creature will stick its head out one end to grab another piece of construction material. Some varieties will use bits of plant, pebbles, or even tiny snails.

A **backswimmer** is a wild scuba diver. That silvery flash at the end of its body is an air bubble, a reserve tank for use until it can get back to the surface. When it's time for a refill, the backswimmer stops paddling and the bubble floats the bug to the surface.

# FIRST AID

**S**ummer activities bring fun and sometimes cuts, stings, bruises, and, of course, sunburn. Become the summer medic by preparing a first-aid kit.

Put the first-aid supplies described at the right in a plastic container with a tight-fitting lid. Keep the first-aid kit in one place—such as on top of the refrigerator—so it will be easy to find. Refill with new supplies as needed and enjoy the summer! Don't forget to bring the kit when hiking or camping.

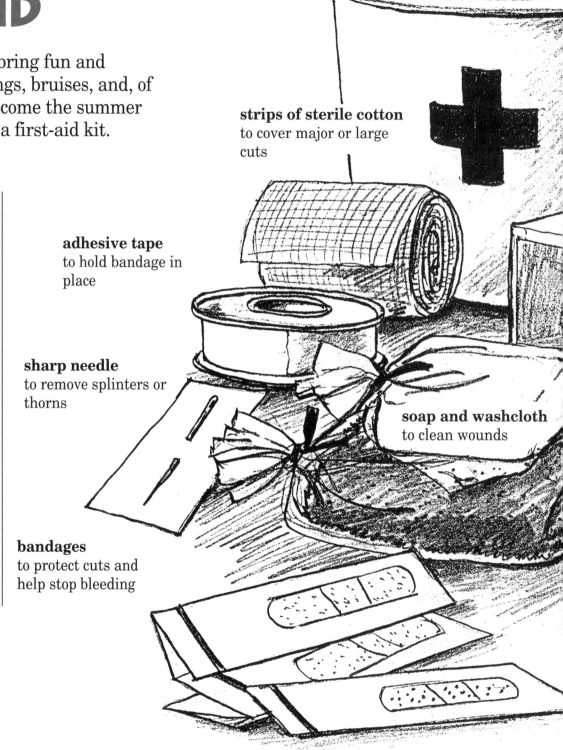

**strips of sterile cotton**
to cover major or large cuts

**adhesive tape**
to hold bandage in place

**sharp needle**
to remove splinters or thorns

**soap and washcloth**
to clean wounds

**bandages**
to protect cuts and help stop bleeding

28

**baking soda–and–water paste**
to take the sting out of wasp and bee stings and to relieve sunburn

**coins and emergency numbers**
to make phone calls

**matches**
to sterilize needle by burning

## SAFETY ALERT

Hippos and elephants know to cover themselves with mud to protect their skin from the sun's ultraviolet rays. Your skin needs protection, too. Wear a sun hat and, when possible, loose long-sleeved, long-legged clothing. Hold clothes up to the light. If you can see through them, the sun's rays can travel through them. It's best to wear baggy, tightly woven cotton. Also, use a good sunscreen and cover sensitive skin with a total block, such as zinc oxide ointment, which acts just like the mud on the hippo.

# WATERFRONT SAFETY

**A**long with water fun goes water safety. Learn the following water safety rules and make a poster to hang at home or in the boathouse.

**1.**
Always swim with a buddy.

**2.**
Find out where the water is a safe depth for swimming. Walk out to check the depth, then swim in.

**3.**
Swim parallel to the shore, never straight out into deep water.

**4.**
Dive only into deep water. Never dive into rocky shallows or unknown waters.

**5.**
Keep clear of boats and water-skiers.

**6.**
Use inflatable tubes and toys with care. Currents and wind can quickly blow you into deep water.

**7.**
Keep the beach clean. Never throw glass or cans into the lake.

**8.**
Keep life jackets and a reach pole or paddle handy for rescues.

## SAFETY ALERT

Even if you weigh only 75 pounds, you can rescue an adult swimmer struggling close to shore. Hold onto one end of the reach pole and, lying at an angle flat on the dock or shore, reach out to the swimmer. Never swim out—a frantic swimmer can pull you under. Do not attempt this rescue without some life-saving training.

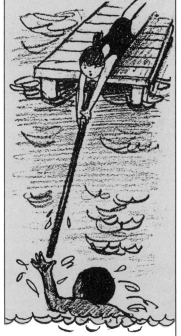

# SWIM GAMES

# MARCO POLO

**M**any land games can be adapted to the water, and waterproof toys can be taken into the lake and enjoyed there, too. So put together a team, get wet, and have fun.

This game requires three or more players.

**1.**
Decide on the playing area for the game—such as from the boat to the dock, or to the sand bar. You'll need an area about the size of a big swimming pool.

**2.**
One person is It and must keep his or her eyes shut.

**3.**
It calls out "Marco." All other players must reply "Polo." It keeps calling out "Marco," swimming toward the nearest Polo, trying to catch one. The other players try to swim away without attracting It's attention. They aren't allowed to dive underwater.

**4.**
The person who is It is allowed to call out "Submarine" and swim underwater with eyes open. It must close his or her eyes after resurfacing. It is allowed only two "submarines," so save them up for when they are really needed.

**5.**
As soon as It touches another person, that person becomes It.

# COLORS

This game requires at least three people. It can be played with colors or any other category, such as cars, baseball teams, or birds. The object of the game is to get to the safe zone when the person who is It calls out your color.

**1.**
Determine the boundaries as in Marco Polo. Begin at one end, where the person who is It stands. The safe zone is at the other end.

**2.**
It stands facing away from the water, on the shore, dock, or diving board.

**3.**
The other players stand in the water or tread water in a line close to the person who is It.

**4.**
Each of the players in the water thinks of a color and whispers it to a neighbor or is on the honor system and keeps it secret. Don't let the person who is It hear the color.

**5.**
The person who is It starts by calling out colors: "Red, blue, turquoise . . . " The other players listen for their colors, and when they hear theirs, they have to swim quickly out to the safe zone.

**6.**
As soon as It hears someone move in the water, he or she turns around, jumps in, and tries to catch the fleeing player.

**7.**
If a player is caught before reaching the safe zone, that player becomes It.

# UNDERWATER GOLF COURSE

As any golfer will attest, golf balls sink. They are perfect to dive for. Just remember the safety rules when diving for anything. Never dive into unknown water, and watch out for rocks.

**You'll need:**

| |
|---|
| 9 empty plastic bottles with handles and caps |
| permanent markers |
| scissors |
| nylon clothesline rope |
| 9 heavy rocks |
| 9 golf balls |
| a pail |

**1.**
Collect nine plastic bottles with caps. Peel off the labels so they don't come off in the water. Label each bottle, using permanent marker, 1 through 9.

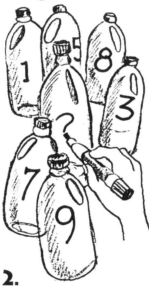

**2.**
Set up the golf course in the water, spacing each "hole" about sixteen feet apart, using the numbered bottles as markers. At the first hole, measure the depth of the water, using your body as a measuring tape. Back on land, cut a piece of rope that will reach the bottom, allowing extra rope for tying knots. Tie the rope to a rock at one end and bottle 1 at the other. Drop the rock in the water to make the first hole.

**3.**
Continue to set up the course until all the bottle markers are floating in the water.

**4.**
Place a golf ball beside each anchor rock and the course is set.

**5.**
The object of the golf game is to swim the course as fast as possible, gathering all nine golf balls. If you can't carry all nine or stuff them in your bathing suit, swim to shore and drop them in a pail. Challenge a friend to see who can do it the fastest. Collect the golf balls after each game so that the waves and current don't steal them.

# WATER BASKETBALL

With your own private basketball hoop, you can play by yourself or take turns with a friend.

**You'll need:**

| |
|---|
| a hammer |
| a dock and an old tire |
| 2 or 3 large nails |
| a beachball |
| an adult helper |

**1.**
Ask an adult to help hammer the tire to the dock using two or three large nails. Position the tire so that it will be above your head while treading water. Choose the side of the dock opposite from where the boat lands or people swim.

**2.**
Inflate a beachball and swim several feet away from the tire "hoop," and take shots at it.

**3.**
See how many baskets you can sink in a minute. Take shots from various angles. Try a slam dunk. Players don't have to be tall to score in water basketball.

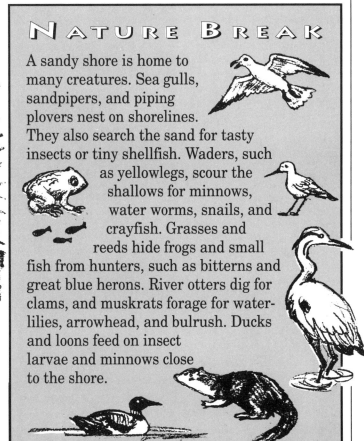

## NATURE BREAK

A sandy shore is home to many creatures. Sea gulls, sandpipers, and piping plovers nest on shorelines. They also search the sand for tasty insects or tiny shellfish. Waders, such as yellowlegs, scour the shallows for minnows, water worms, snails, and crayfish. Grasses and reeds hide frogs and small fish from hunters, such as bitterns and great blue herons. River otters dig for clams, and muskrats forage for water-lilies, arrowhead, and bulrush. Ducks and loons feed on insect larvae and minnows close to the shore.

# MAKE A SNORKEL

**L**egs splashing, hands paddling, bathing suits bobbing—people playing in the water may seem strange to fish. Get a fish-eye view by making a snorkel.

| You'll need: |
| --- |
| a long stalk of horsetail (it's also called scouring rush—see the box on the next page) |
| a swimming mask |

**1.**
Pick a long stem of horsetail. Pull off the cone and pinch all the joints.

**2.**
Blow and inhale carefully through the stem until there is a clear airway.

**3.**
Put on the swimming mask and carry the rush snorkel into the water. Find a steady place and slowly put your head under the water.

**4.**
Put the snorkel into your mouth and direct it in a long arch up into the air. Blow any water out and breathe in, carefully at first, making sure not to suck water. Then breathe, watch, and listen.

## HORSETAIL

Horsetail (also called scouring rush and horsepipe) grows in patches on sandy banks and moist slopes. It has a finely grooved, dark green stem with no branches and a small cone at the top. The stem is divided evenly into segments, each with a skirt of green and black teeth at the joints. In dinosaur times, plants similar to it grew as tall as a ten-story building. But now horsetails grow to be only about five feet tall.

Plains Indians once used them to make brooms and mats. Ojibwa people and European pioneers scrubbed and cleaned their kettles and pans with this plant. For making a snorkel, the important feature of the horsetail is that it's hollow.

## UNDERWATER SOUNDS

When breathing underwater with the horsetail snorkel, listen. Are the sounds recognizable? Try shuffling rocks on the bottom. Sound travels faster underwater and seems to be much louder. Get your head out of the water if you hear something as noisy as a motorboat!

# HAND-PADDLED RAFT

**O**n sweltering days, it's best to stay in the water a long time. Take a break from swimming in a hand-paddled raft.

| You'll need: |
| --- |
| an adult helper |
| 3 car tire inner tubes (ask at a gas station for used, patched, inflated tire inner tubes) |
| a board just longer than three inner tubes |
| a handsaw |
| sandpaper |
| paint and paintbrush (optional) |
| a pencil |
| a drill |
| a 32-foot nylon rope |
| one life jacket per person |
| a ruler |

**1.**

Ask an adult to help cut the sharp corners off the board with the handsaw and sand all sides of the board, including the edges and the corners.

**2.**

Line up the inner tubes on the board and mark where they touch the board. Use the ruler to draw lines as shown (four lines per tube).

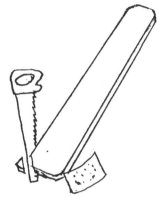

**3.**

Remove tubes and ask the adult to drill two holes on every line (twenty-four holes), the same distance from the edge of board. Sand around the holes.

**4.**

If you want to paint the board, this is the time to do it. Wait until the paint dries before continuing.

**5.**

With the tubes lined up on the board, lace the nylon rope through the holes, over the tubes and under the board to bind the tubes to the board.

**6.**

Knot the beginning and end of the rope so the tubes stay secure.

**7.**

Put on a bathing suit and life jacket and head to the beach. Launch the raft board-side up. Sit with legs dangling into the water over the board or lie along the length of the board. Paddle and direct the raft with your hands.

## THE BIG TUBE

It's always worth a stop by the municipal or township road maintenance shed to ask if they have any used inner tubes from their road graders, monster gravel trucks, or earth movers. A local farmer might have an old tractor tire inner tube. These gigantic inner tubes can be patched and filled with air at a gas station. They make terrific, huge floating toys—even in the shallowest water.

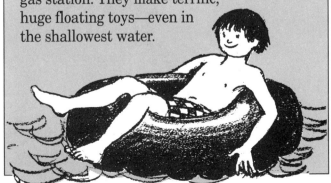

# DIVING RAFT

**S**ome people think every cottage needs a raft just as much as it needs a sink, a stove, a toilet, or beds. Ask around for any construction leftovers—and some help—to make a diving raft.

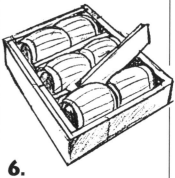

| You'll need: |
| --- |
| sandpaper |
| a full sheet of 1/2-inch to 3/4-inch plywood |
| a drill with large and small drill bits |
| wood planking about 6 inches wide by 1 inch deep and enough length to run around the outside of the plywood twice (the planking can be several pieces) |
| a handsaw |
| a screwdriver |
| wood screws about 4 inches long |
| empty, sealed, small barrels or leftover Styrofoam insulation |
| marine paint and paintbrush |
| a heavy, flat rock for an anchor |
| a 16-foot rope |
| a pencil |
| a ruler |
| an adult helper |

**1.**
Sand the plywood completely.

**2.**
Ask an adult to drill a three-quarter-inch hole in one end of the wood planking for the anchor. Sand each piece of planking completely.

**3.**
The finished raft will be very heavy. Assemble the materials at a flat working area close to the beach.

**4.**
Line up the wood planks under the plywood at a right angle, flush to the edges.

**5.**
Screw through the top of the plywood into the planks, all around the edge of the plywood. It's easier if you first drill a narrow hole for the screw to follow.

**6.**
Flip the raft over. Measure and saw the remaining planks into lengths to form tight frames around the barrels or insulation. Mark on the sides of the raft where the frames meet the sides. Turn the raft over. Continue

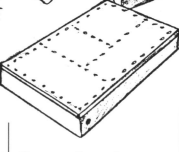

the pencil marks onto the top of the raft.

Screw the plywood into the frames using the pencil lines as guides.

## 7.

Paint the top and sides. Let it dry.

## 8.

Tie the rope to the rock with a clove hitch. (See Anchor Rock on page 47.) Lay the rock in the center of raft and run the line through the anchor hole.

## 9.

With the help of at least one adult, paddle the raft to where you want it to float. The water under the raft must be free of rocks in all directions and at least thirteen feet deep.

## 10.

Hold the free end of the rope and drop the anchor. When it hits bottom, tie off the end you're holding, leaving a little slack so it is easy to untie the raft and float to shore.

## ECOWATCH

When Styrofoam is manufactured and when it is burned at a dump, gases are released that may pollute the air and contribute to the greenhouse effect. Using leftovers in a diving raft is a way to reuse it instead of sending it to the dump. However, if there isn't any around, don't go out and buy it specifically for the raft. Instead, use empty, sealed barrels or large containers used to hold roofing tar or cement block sealants. Look for containers the same size.

## DIVING

Watch a kingfisher, a tern, or an otter dive. Head first, they slip into the water with hardly a splash. When people dive, they have to lift their feet up and over from a standing position. Always dive with arms outstretched in front—it looks better and also provides protection against head injury.

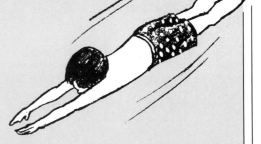

# CANOE TIPS AND STROKES

**U**se a canoe as a means of transportation, just like the voyageurs did two hundred years ago. That requires good, strong strokes. Or put a sweatshirt over the handles of two paddles, stick them between the gunwales, catch the wind, and canoe-sail down the lake.

To canoe, learn the proper strokes and how to get in and out of the canoe without getting wet. A calm day without wind or waves is best for practicing. Grab a life jacket and ask an adult or friend to come along.

## THE ANATOMY OF A CANOE

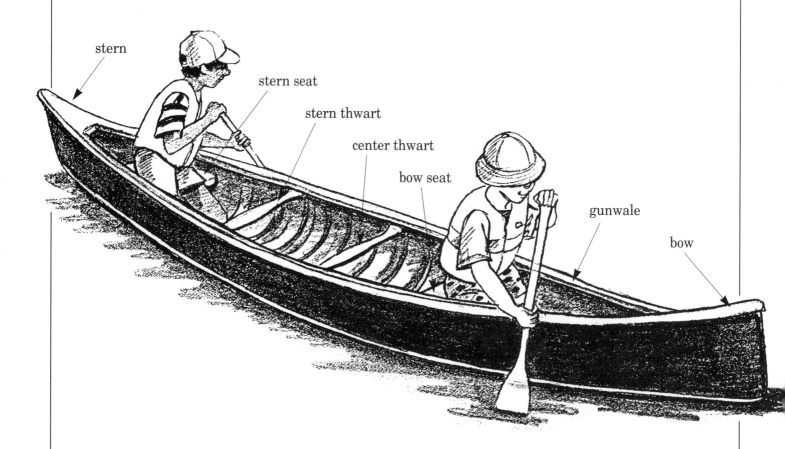

stern
stern seat
stern thwart
center thwart
bow seat
gunwale
bow

## ACCESSORIES

Everyone in the canoe needs the right size paddle. Choose a paddle that is no higher than your chin. You'll also need a certified life jacket and you may want a kneeling pad or cushion. Don't forget a sun hat or sunscreen.

## GETTING IN AND OUT

Decide first who will be in the bow and who in the stern. The bowperson must watch for rocks, shallows, and other obstacles while paddling. The sternperson steers.

If you leap into a canoe as if it were a power boat, the canoe will tip you out in a flash. Approach a canoe with caution.

The bowperson gets in first while the sternperson holds the gunwale to steady the canoe. When boarding, grip the paddle with two hands and hold it across your waist.

Step into the center of the middle section, where the bottom is flat.

Place the paddle across the gunwales and bend your knees for balance.

Now proceed to the bow, crawling over the thwarts slowly, using the paddle across the gunwales to keep steady.

The sternperson gets in last while the bowperson steadies the canoe, either by driving the paddle into the bottom of the lake or by holding onto the dock or shore.

Get out of a canoe in the opposite order—the sternperson gets out first and the bowperson follows carefully.

# CANOE STROKES

There are four parts to any stroke: the catch, pull, recovery, and feather.

## THE STRAIGHT STROKE

Grip the paddle handle in one hand at shoulder level near your nose. Grasp the shaft with your other hand just above the blade, keeping arm straight.

Dip the blade into the water. *Catch* by pushing the handle away from your nose toward the opposite knee.

Thrust your upper arm out straight as you *pull* your lower arm past your hip.

Bend your lower elbow to lift the paddle out of the water behind you (*recovery*).

Rotate the paddle on its side or across your stomach (*feather*) and return to catch position.

Repeat the steps in a steady rhythm. Try to use all muscles in the upper body when paddling. If you use just the arm muscles, your arms will get tired quickly.

## THE J-STROKE

The J-stroke is a steering stroke. It differs from the straight stroke only at the end of the pull. When the paddle has passed the hip, the sternperson bends the wrists, rotating the paddle. The blade is now parallel to the boat. The pull draws a J in the water.

45

# KEEP YOUR BOAT AFLOAT

**H**ere's how to keep a boat shipshape. With a trim boat and a knowledge of boat safety, the summer will be smooth sailing.

## WITHOUT KEYS, YOU'RE SUNK

If you need to carry a key while on boat trips, a floating key chain can come in handy.

| You'll need: |
| --- |
| a corkscrew |
| a cork |
| twist ties |
| a key |

**1.**
Using a corkscrew, enlarge the hole in the middle of a cork by twisting in the corkscrew at both ends. Hold the cork up to the light to check that the hole reaches all the way through the cork.

**2.**
Insert one large plastic twist tie or two small twist ties joined together through the hole in the cork.

**3.**
Thread the key onto one end and twist the ties together.

**4.**
Test for buoyancy in a sink filled with water. If it sinks, try a larger cork or add another.

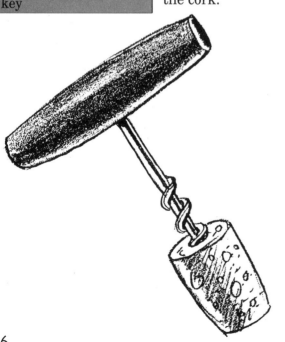

# ANCHOR ROCK

When you're out exploring and you want to moor for a swim or a picnic, an anchor rock will come in handy.

**You'll need:**

a large, flat, square rock

a 65-foot nylon rope

**1.**
Look for an anchor rock that you're able to lift yourself.

**2.**
Tie one end of the rope around the rock, as you would a package. Make the rope secure by tying a clove hitch knot. (See page 203.)

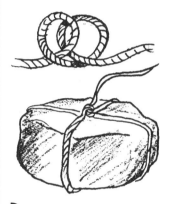

**3.**
Coil the remaining rope neatly and lay it on top of the rock.

**4.**
Place the anchor in the stern of the boat before each expedition.

**5.**
Secure the loose end of the rope to a cleat on the boat or to the seat of a canoe, using a double half hitch knot. (See page 203.)

**6.**
Before leaving a boat, tug the rope to check that the anchor is secure. In shallow water, haul in and tighten extra rope so the boat doesn't drift.

# SAILOR'S BAILER

If it rains or you are sprayed with waves, a bailer will help keep the boat from swamping (filling with water and sinking). Modify a plastic jug to make a bailer that won't rust.

**You'll need:**

| You'll need: |
| --- |
| a pen |
| a large plastic jug with a handle and cap |
| a sharp knife or scissors |
| an adult helper |

**1.**
Using the pen, draw a line halfway around the jug about two inches from the bottom, up to the middle, around the middle below the handle, and back down to the line around the bottom.

**2.**
Hold the jug by the handle and carefully cut along the line.

**3.**
Make sure the cap of the jug is tightly fastened.

**4.**
Sit in the back of the boat so your weight will lower the boat's stern. Hold the jug by the handle to scoop out any water in the boat.

**5.**
Keep the bailer handy in one place in the boat.

SHORESIDE

# BOAT
## RULE BOX

The following should always be kept in a boat—some are required by law, some are sensible precautions.

**1.**
One government-approved life jacket or floating cushion for each passenger.

**2.**
One sailor's bailer. (See page 48.)

**3.**
In case of motorboat engine failure, two oars or paddles.

**4.**
One first-aid kit in a waterproof container. (See page 28.)

**5.**
Keep a flashlight with the emergency kit for signaling for help. See the box on this page to learn the Morse code signal.

**6.**
Turn to page 42 for canoe tips.

## SIGNAL FOR HELP

Watch the water for the twinkling lights of boats. Would you be able to tell if boat passengers were in distress and were signaling for help? Engine failure in a power boat and lack of wind for sailboats are common crises on lakes. If you see a light flashing in a repeated pattern, pay attention. The international Morse code signal for HELP! is three short blinks, three long blinks, then three short blinks, followed by a pause and a repetition of the signal.

· · · — — — · · ·

If someone is calling for help, get an adult and go to the rescue if it is safe or telephone the police for help. Larger lakes have police launches, or the police will ask local boaters for help.

## ECO WATCH

Help keep the lake alive and clean by thinking about everything added to the lake. If you must use a motorboat, keep joyriding to a minimum and have a destination in mind. If you have oars, use them—it's better for you and for the lake. Canoeing, sailing, and windsurfing don't pollute, and allow a closer look at the shoreline and what lives there. Don't throw any junk or garbage into the lake. Make sure to clean with phosphate-free detergents or pure soap, and never dump soapy water directly into the lake.

49

# MAKE A WATERSCOPE

**O**n the edges of most lakes, you can find shallow reedy marshes to explore. Make a waterscope to get a close-up look at the creatures living there. Paddle the boat over to the reeds and peer in.

| You'll need: |
| --- |
| a knife |
| a large plastic container such as an ice cream or yogurt container |
| clear plastic wrap |
| a strong rubber band |

**1.**
Ask an adult to help cut the bottom out of the plastic container.

**2.**
Stretch clear plastic wrap over the bottom and secure it with a strong rubber band.

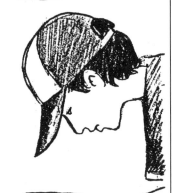

**3.**
Lower the plastic-covered end into the water. It should be watertight so that you can hold it a few inches into the water and get a clear view of what's down there.

Point the waterscope under a water lily. Look for bass hiding in the leafy shadow and along the stem toward the muddy bottom.

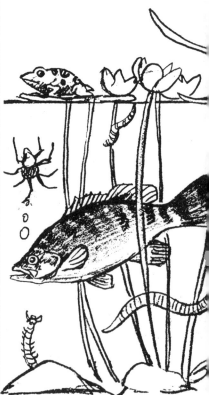

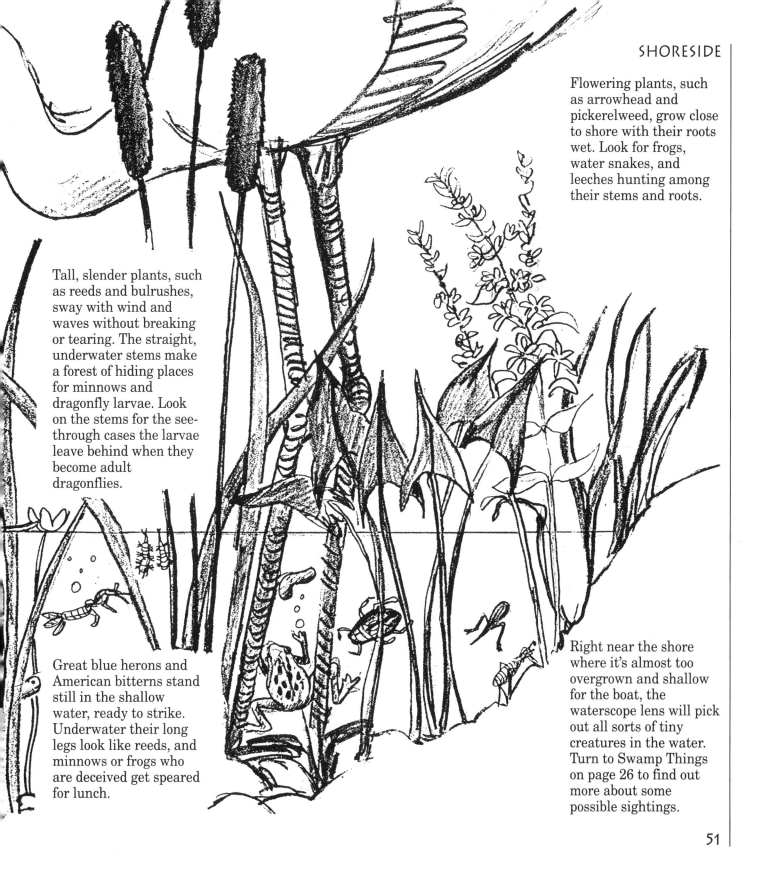

Flowering plants, such as arrowhead and pickerelweed, grow close to shore with their roots wet. Look for frogs, water snakes, and leeches hunting among their stems and roots.

Tall, slender plants, such as reeds and bulrushes, sway with wind and waves without breaking or tearing. The straight, underwater stems make a forest of hiding places for minnows and dragonfly larvae. Look on the stems for the see-through cases the larvae leave behind when they become adult dragonflies.

Great blue herons and American bitterns stand still in the shallow water, ready to strike. Underwater their long legs look like reeds, and minnows or frogs who are deceived get speared for lunch.

Right near the shore where it's almost too overgrown and shallow for the boat, the waterscope lens will pick out all sorts of tiny creatures in the water. Turn to Swamp Things on page 26 to find out more about some possible sightings.

51

# LANDSIDE

Turn inland and there's tons to do.
Fly a kite or construct a flagpole,
build a fort or a bluebird house, track
time or maybe snakes, net bugs, or
investigate an anthill. Or simply
make a hammock and lie down with a
good book and a refreshing drink.

# SWING INTO SUMMER

**N**o cottage is complete without a swing or two. On hot days, they create wind to blow through your hair. When you're mad or glad, shout or sing as you swing.

## STEEL-BELTED FUN

**You'll need:**

| |
|---|
| a tire or inner tube |
| a strong 10-foot rope |
| a ladder |
| a sturdy tree limb |
| an adult helper |

**1.**

Look around for an old tire or take a trip to the dump. Choose a tire that isn't ripped, studded, or chained. If you want a soft swing, ask the mechanic at a garage for an old inner tube. Inflate it at the garage or use it floppy.

**2.**

Ask an adult to help choose a site for the swing. The tree has to be located away from buildings, electrical wires, and roads.

**3.**

Tie a loop knot around the tire (see page 203). With a ladder and help from an adult, tie the rope to a strong right-angled branch at least a yard from the trunk using a double half hitch. (See page 203.)

**4.**

The tire should swing about three feet above the ground. Get swinging!

# BOARD SWING

**You'll need:**

| |
|---|
| a 12-by-20-inch board |
| a saw |
| a drill |
| sandpaper |
| strong rope |
| a ladder |
| a sturdy tree limb |
| an adult helper |

**1.**

Ask an adult to help cut the board to the required measurements using a handsaw.

**2.**

Choose a drill bit a little thicker than the rope. Ask the adult helper to drill a hole in the middle of each end of the board about four inches from the edge.

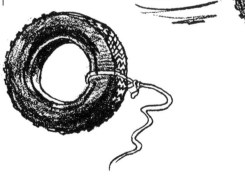

# TARZAN ROPE

**3.**

Using medium sandpaper, sand the board so you won't get any splinters. Make sure to sand well along the edges.

**4.**

Thread the rope up through one hole, run it along the bottom of the swing, and thread it down through the other hole. Pull the rope through until there are equal lengths of rope on both sides.

**5.**

Choose a site for the swing, as in the tire swing. Tie both ropes on the tree branch, using double half hitches. (See page 203.) Allow about twenty to thirty inches clearance above the ground for your legs.

| You'll need: |
| --- |
| an 8-foot rope at least $3/4$ inch thick |
| a sturdy tree limb |
| a ladder |

**1.**

Tie shoelace knots in the rope fifteen inches apart. The knots will help you climb up.

**2.**

Choose a site as you did for the tire swing.

**3.**

Tie the rope to the branch of the swing tree using a loop knot. (See page 203.)

**4.**

Wrap your legs around one of the knots, hold on tight, and kick off from the tree.

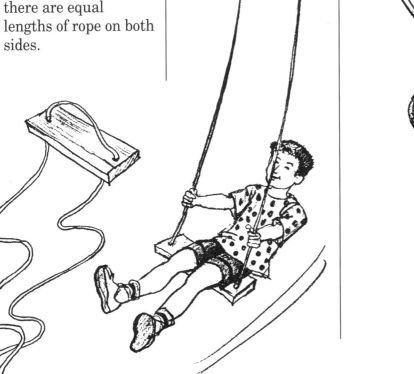

55

# VEGETABLE GARDEN

If you like to have a say in the menu, start a vegetable garden and grow what you like to eat! This project needs care for most of the summer.

| You'll need: |
| --- |
| a round-mouth shovel |
| peat moss and/or compost |
| vegetable seeds |
| string and a ruler |
| sticks for stakes |
| a hoe or garden rake |
| a hose and water |

**1.**

Choose a sunny spot within reach of the hose for the garden. Plant stakes around the boundaries—seven feet by ten feet will be enough for starters. Check with an adult to make sure it's all right to dig there.

**2.**
Remove the grass with the round-mouth shovel. Use the sod to patch bare spots on the rest of the lawn.

**3.**
Prepare the soil by turning over the entire area, chopping up and loosening it with each shovelful. Dig in peat moss and/or compost to break up and enrich the soil.

**4.**
Choose vegetable seeds that germinate quickly and have a short growing season. Look on the back of seed packets for the information about each variety. Peas, lettuce, beans, spinach, and Swiss chard are all good selections. Buy chives and marigold seeds for pest control. Avoid carrots, beets, pumpkin, and zucchini, which all require a long growing season, unless you are able to plant them in May or early June.

**5.**

Mark garden rows by tying the string across the plot to the stakes. Leave at least a foot between rows. You'll need the space for walking and weeding, and the plants need space to grow. Using a hoe or the corner of a rake, dig a trough for each variety of seed.

**6.**

Follow the directions on each pack of seeds because the depth for planting varies from vegetable to vegetable. Cover the seeds with soil and tap lightly. Plant the chives and marigold seeds around the edges of the garden. Insects and small animals don't like the smell of these plants and are less likely to help themselves to the garden.

**7.**

After planting, water the entire garden well. Soak the soil with a gentle sprinkle, which will not dislodge the seeds.

**8.**

Water the garden regularly and generously. The summer heat can dry out and kill the seedlings and plants. It's best to water in the early morning or in the evening—when the sun is low in the sky, less water will evaporate. Weed once a week.

**9.**

While waiting for the plants to peek above the soil, make some of the safe wildlife deterrents described on the next two pages.

# MAKE A **SCARECROW**

Rabbits, deer, and raccoons are likely to share some of the garden food, but a scarecrow and several pinwheels should help you keep most of the crop.

**You'll need:**

a hammer and nails

a 7-foot-long piece of 2-by-4-inch wood—most people will know what you mean if you ask for a two-by-four

a board for the arms

a plastic bag

newspaper

string

a permanent marker

a large old shirt

wild grasses, a sun hat, or other things to decorate the scarecrow

**1.**
Nail the two pieces of wood into a T shape.

**2.**
Hammer the T upright into the soil of the garden.

**3.**
Fill the plastic bag with scrunched-up newspaper. Tie it closed with a piece of string.

**4.**
Draw a fierce face on the plastic bag.

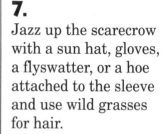

**5.**
Fasten the head to the top of the T with string around the neck.

**6.**
Using the crossbar of the T as arms, dress the scarecrow with a shirt. The flapping shirttails will frighten away some animals.

**7.**
Jazz up the scarecrow with a sun hat, gloves, a flyswatter, or a hoe attached to the sleeve and use wild grasses for hair.

# PEST-CONTROL PINWHEELS

**You'll need:**

- a thin 6-by-6-inch piece of plastic (plastic covers for school reports will do)
- a ballpoint pen
- a ruler
- scissors
- a thumbtack with a long needle
- a chopstick or thin, straight stick

**1.**
Mark the center of the plastic square with the pen. Number the four corners, starting with the top left corner and continuing clockwise.

**2.**
Draw a faint X through the midpoint of the square, joining 1 and 3 with one line and 2 and 4 with another.

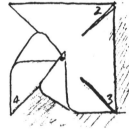

**3.**
Measure and mark the halfway point between the midpoint and each corner. Cut to this point from each corner.

**4.**
Fold the lower half of corner 1 to the midpoint, followed by the lower half of corner 4, the upper half of corner 3, and the upper half of corner 2.

**5.**
Push a tack through all four corners at the midpoint of the square and into the stick.

Place some pinwheels around the garden or attach to the scarecrow. The click they make will scare away small animals and birds.

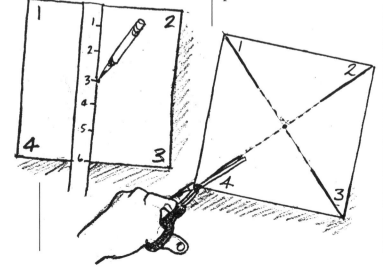

# SUMMER GARBAGE

**E**ven in the summer, it's possible to reduce, reuse, and recycle. Make the cottage "greener" by building a composter to convert waste from the kitchen into food for the soil.

Build a solid structure that can hold the waste, heat up, let in air, keep out pesky creatures, and have an opening for stirring and scooping out the compost. Try to make one without buying any materials. Here are some design ideas.

## MINI COMPOSTER

To start small, use an old, large, rectangular laundry basket. With a nail and hammer, make drainage holes in the bottom. For a lid, use a piece of plywood bigger than the basket. Put a large, heavy rock on top to keep out raccoons. Place in a sunny spot away from the cottage or picnic areas.

## IT'S A PIT

Select a site for the composting pit. Check with an adult before starting to dig—you don't want to unearth cables or a septic tank. Dig a hole of about a square yard and up to a yard deep. An old window screen makes a good lid. It lets in moisture, lets out smells, and keeps out compost thieves. If a screen is not heavy enough, place a rock on top.

# THE CARPENTER'S COMPOSTER

If you are good with a hammer and nails, ask an adult to help make this wooden composter. Using two-by-fours, make a frame one yard square and one yard tall. The sides can be covered with lattice, plywood with holes drilled in it, or chicken wire. A heavy square of plywood makes a good lid. Don't forget the rock "lock."

## COMPOST CUISINE

Perfect compost needs ingredients from the beach, the lawn, the kitchen, and the garden. Place a layer of beach stones on the bottom of the composter or the pit. Next comes a layer of grass cuttings, leaves, or trimmings from a hedge or bush. Then add a layer of kitchen waste. Compost all vegetable matter, coffee grounds, tea bags, eggshells, and unbleached paper. (Don't put in meat, dressings, cereal, or dairy products —they smell and attract flies and larger creatures.) Top with a shovelful of soil. Sprinkle with water and stir. Continue to feed and stir the composter all summer long.

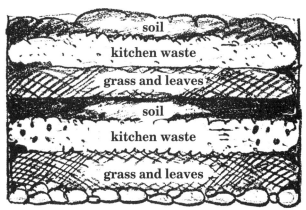

The compost will have to "cook" for about a year. It's like a good stew—it needs to simmer and mix its flavors for a long time. But the garden will be hungry for compost goodness next spring. Shovel the compost, which looks like rich, black soil, onto the flower or vegetable garden. Dig it in before planting time. Compost can also be used to enrich hanging baskets or planters.

# MAKE YOUR OWN HAMMOCK

**T**here is nothing like a hammock on a lazy, hazy summer day. Read or stare at the clouds while lolling in the folds of a hammock. It is simple to make. The tough part will be finding the hammock empty so you can have a turn.

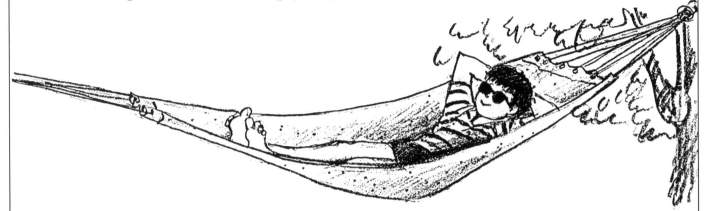

| You'll need: |
| --- |
| a sturdy cotton sheet, twin size |
| straight pins |
| a sewing needle and polyester thread |
| a measuring tape |
| a dime |
| a pencil |
| heavy-duty thread |
| a large sewing needle |
| a thimble (optional) |
| scissors |
| 2 trees about 8 feet apart |
| a 165-foot clothesline rope |
| 2 large tethering rings (available at hardware stores) |
| 2 sturdy screw hooks |
| an adult helper |

**1.**

Fold the ends of the sheet over at the hem. Pin with straight pins.

**2.**

Using the polyester thread and the smaller sewing needle, sew the folded ends with a blanket stitch. (See page 205.)

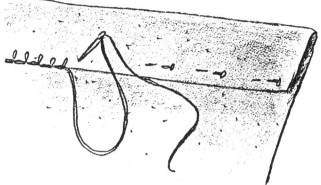

**3.**

At each end, measure the width of the sheet and find the center. Mark it on the hem with a circle, using the dime and pencil. Measure and mark circles at eight-inch intervals to both edges. These circles mark where to make grummets, or reinforced holes, for threading the rope through. This side is the right side of the sheet.

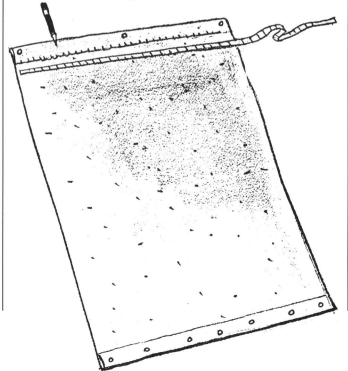

**4.**

Using a yard of heavy-duty thread, thread the large needle, double the thread, and knot the ends together (see page 205).

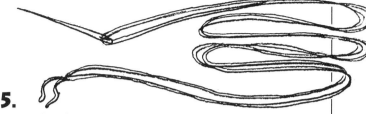

**5.**

To make the grummets, begin by pulling the needle from the wrong side of the sheet into a pencil-marked circle on the right side of the sheet. Sew three-fourths-inch-long stitches all the way around the outside of the circle. Overlapping stiches will make the grummet stronger. Knot the thread when the circle is complete. Repeat for each circle.

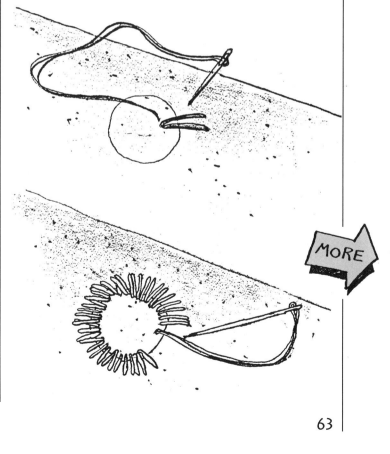

MORE

63

**8.**

Cut one piece of rope for each grummet sewn. The length of each piece should be two and a half times the distance between the end of the hammock and the tree.

**6.**

Using the sharp point of the scissors, open the center of the circle, taking care not to cut the stitching. Repeat this procedure for all the circles.

**7.**

Lay the hammock on the ground between the two trees. Measure the distance from the ends of the hammock to the trees.

## 9.

Thread each rope through the grummets so that it is doubled. Lay one end of each rope under the tethering ring and one over. Tie each to the ring using a square knot. (See page 204.)

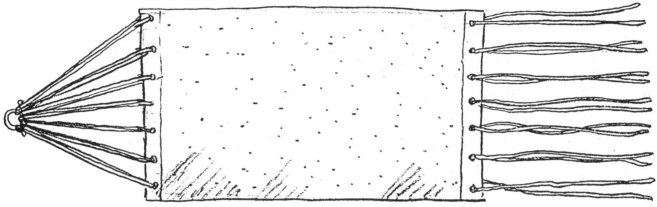

## 10.

Screw one hook into each tree about five feet off the ground. Ask an adult to help.

## 11.

Loop the tethering ring over the hook. Now quickly hop into the hammock before anyone else does.

## 12.

Take the hammock indoors if rain is expected.

# TELLING TIMES

**L**ong before people had watches or clocks, they knew how to tell time. When stomachs growl or eyelids won't stay open, it's either mealtime or bedtime. Make a sundial to tell the time without a watch.

| You'll need: |
|---|
| a sharp pencil |
| a 6-inch piece of string |
| a 12-by-6-inch piece of wood or thick cardboard |
| a piece of thin cardboard, such as the side of a cereal box |
| a ruler |
| scissors |
| white glue |

## 1.

Start by making the base of the sundial. Tie the pencil to one end of the string. Hold the free end of the string under your thumb, in the center of one edge of the piece of wood. Pull the string tight and draw a semi-circle on the wood from the top to the bottom, around your thumb. Then draw a straight line from where you held your thumb to the opposite edge of the wood.

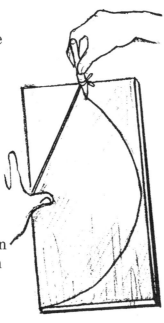

## 2.

Next, make the sundial's "hand," called the gnomon. On the piece of thin cardboard, mark six inches along the bottom and six inches up the side. Cut diagonally between the two marks to make a triangle.

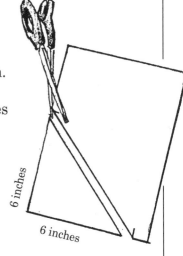

6 inches

6 inches

## 3.

On one side, draw a straight line a half-inch up from the edge and fold along that line to make a flap. You should now have a triangular card with a flap on the bottom.

## 4.

Glue the flap onto the base as shown, so that the crease sits on the straight line in the center of the board.

**5.**

Place the sundial on a flat spot outside where the sun will shine on it all day. Face it so the gnomon points north. (On a clear night, find north by pointing the gnomon toward the North Star. The North Star is easy to find because it's the one that is "pouring" out of the Big Dipper.)

**6.**

Next make the dial. Every hour, mark where the gnomon's shadow falls on the base. Label each mark with the hour. Continue until the hours from sunup to sundown are marked. Now you can leave your watch inside on sunny days and read the time from the sundial. Make sure it stays in exactly the same spot.

## NATURAL WATCHES

Just as people have an inner clock to tell when it's lunchtime or bedtime, so do some plants. Learn to read these natural clocks.

Marigold flowers, for instance, open each day at 7:00 A.M. Blue chicory and pickerelweed close up at noon. The white water lily shuts tight at 4:00 P.M. each day and the marigold closes by 7:00 P.M. Look around to find other examples of plant clocks to help you tell the time.

CHICORY

PICKERELWEED

Some plants open on schedule every day even if it's not sunny. Cover a plant clock with a pail and peek in to see if it still opens and closes on time, even in the dark.

Look for animal clocks, too. Deerflies may annoy after 9:00 A.M., horseflies at 2:00 P.M., and pesky mosquitoes by 8:00 P.M. Bees can be taught to tell you the time. If you put honey on a spoon in the same place at the same time every day, bees will learn to expect it and come buzzing—and they won't be late.

# FLAGPOLE

**R**aising and flying a flag can become a summer tradition. Make a personal flag, incorporating classic symbols such as lions and crowns or imaginative designs that reflect a hobby. A flagpole can be used as a signal to friends: when the red flag is waving, stay away; when the green flag is up, come on over. So get some helpers together and hoist a flagpole.

| You'll need: |
| --- |
| an ax |
| a 23-to-32-foot cedar tree |
| a pruning saw |
| 2 sheets coarse sandpaper |
| a sharp knife |
| a 65-foot ½-inch nylon rope |
| a 1- or 1½-inch pulley |
| a shovel |
| a pail of gravel |
| a cleat |
| a flag |
| a screwdriver |
| an adult helper |

**1.**
With help from an adult, select and cut down a tall, slim, straight tree with a base diameter of about six inches. Cedar will last longest but poplar or beech will work, too.

**2.**
Using a pruning saw, trim all the branches close to the trunk.

**3.**
After pruning, use coarse sandpaper to buff off the roughness.

**4.**
If you choose to skin off the bark, go slowly. Use a very sharp knife, always stroking away from the body. Hold the knife at a forty-five-degree angle, cutting to remove the bark without gouging the wood. Cedar bark will peel off in strips once started with the knife. (See Knife Safety on page 117.)

**5.**
Attach the pulley about twenty inches from the top of the pole. Do this before hoisting the pole.

**6.**
Thread the rope through the pulley. Tie a loose knot to keep it from coming out while you raise the pole.

**7.**
Choose a site for the flagpole that is out in the open and away from telephone and electrical lines.

MORE

## 8.

Using a shovel and lots of muscle, dig a hole about one yard deep. The width of the hole will depend on the size of the butt (the wider end) of the tree.

## 9.

To raise the flagpole, have one person hold the butt steady over the hole. The other person picks up the pole near the pulley and walks toward the hole, raising the pole hand over hand. (Push the pole ahead of the body, using your chest and shoulders to support the weight of the pole.) Meanwhile, the first person steers the butt of the pole so it slips easily into the hole.

## 10.

Then one person holds the pole straight in place while the other pours a pail of gravel into the hole, then shovels back the soil. Both use feet to tap down the soil firmly.

## 11.

At about chest level, screw the cleat onto the pole.

70

**12.**
Because a flag must be secured at the top and bottom, the top of a flag usually has a toggle and the bottom has a small rope coming out of a grummet (a reinforced ring). Stand at the flagpole and figure out which end of the flag is up.

**13.**
Untie the nylon rope on the flagpole and attach the flag to the toggle using a clove hitch. (See page 203.)

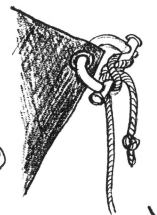

**14.**
Let the flag hang down and secure the other end of the rope in the grummet rope, using a sheet bend. (See page 204.)

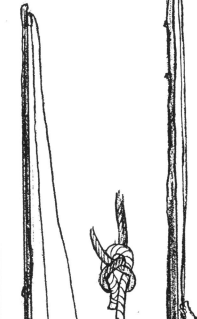

**15.**
Raise the flag to the top of the pole and secure the rope around the cleat.

**16.**
The flag will last longer if taken down during bad weather. Make sure to store it in a dry place during the winter.

## FLAG-FLYING RULES

**1.**
When flying the national flag, it is considered unlucky or unpatriotic to let the flag drag on the ground.

**2.**
Traditionally, the national flag is raised after sunrise and lowered before sunset.

**3.**
When a flag is flying upside down, it signals "Help."

# WILDLIFE BLIND

Seeing an animal up close in its natural habitat can be very exciting. Get a closer, longer look by constructing a wildlife blind beside a marsh, on the beach, in a meadow, or at the edge of the forest.

**You'll need:**

a 10-by-3-foot cloth

scissors and string

camouflage material, such as sticks and leaves

a ruler

**1.**
Choose a site where animals or birds have been seen. Bulrushes, shrubs, tall grasses, or sand dunes are natural hiding places. Avoid areas known as habitat for dangerous animals.

**2.**
Select cloth that will blend in with the site, such as an old piece of burlap, a brown bedspread, or an old green tablecloth.

**3.**
Make holes in the four corners of the cloth with the scissors.

**4.**
Cut four 20-inch pieces of string. Pull a piece of string through each corner opening and knot it to secure it to the cloth.

**5.**
Cut four or five 10-inch slits in the cloth. These will be the peepholes.

**6.**

Wrap the cloth around one side of the bulrushes, shrubs, or tall grasses, close to the ground. Use the strings to secure it in place.

**7.**

Use grasses, sticks, and leaves found around the site to camouflage the blind, making it blend in with the surroundings.

**8.**

If the blind is behind a sand dune, you'll need three sturdy sticks to jab into the sand. Make a V with the sticks, securing the ends of the cloth on the outside two sticks.

**9.**

After several days, the blind will become part of the scenery, and local wildlife will no longer avoid it.

**10.**

Snuggle in behind the blind and quietly wait for any passersby. Use the peepholes to see if there are any wild creatures in the area.

## GAME TRAILS

If you look closely at the ground in meadows or forests, you can see little paths used by animals. These are called game trails. They can be used by all sizes of creatures, from mice to coyotes, to travel safely from the cover of the forest to the nearest watering hole. Try to find a game trail and make the blind within view of it.
What animals travel on the trail? Make sure to stay quiet and still, especially if you see a skunk.

# CALL OF THE WILD

**H**unters attract wildlife by mimicking their sounds. Native people knew how to lure migrating geese close enough to shoot by repeating their honks. Or they could attract moose in dense bush by scraping an antler on spruce bark.

Birds and animals are also attracted by squeaky distress calls. They may be friendly and want to help, they may be just curious, or they may be predators looking for an easy lunch. On a quiet day, make a wildlife caller and see who comes to investigate you.

| You'll need: |
| --- |
| 2 Popsicle sticks |
| a long, wide blade of wild grass (some people use a length of broken cassette tape) |
| a rubber band |

**1.**
Make sure the Popsicle sticks are clean and dry.

**2.**
Sandwich a blade of dry grass between the two Popsicle sticks. Secure one end by wrapping the rubber band around it.

**3.**
Pinch the open end, and blow through the caller as if playing a harmonica.

**4.**
To attract wildlife, sit quietly and blow into the caller repeatedly, at the same rhythm and pitch as a baby crying, *"Waaa waaa waaa."* See what it attracts. Blue jays and chickadees may come first. Keep it up and you may spot a fox or hawk.

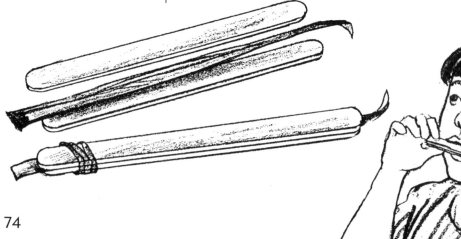

74

# CRY LIKE A LOON

Make the mournful cry of a loon using only your hands and mouth.

## 1.

Hold your hands together loosely as if just starting to clap. Keep that position, leaving an air pocket between the palms, but cup the hands tightly so the air pocket is surrounded.

## 2.

Press your thumbs together so your thumbnails face you. Bend the thumb joints down against your cupped hands. There should be a space below your thumb joints and above the base of your thumbs.

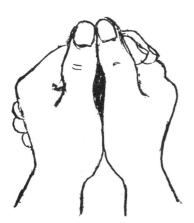

## 3.

Put the thumb joints to your lips, leaving the hole below the joints free to the air.

## 4.

Hold your lips loosely, as if getting ready to whistle. Hold back your tongue a little. Blow silently onto the thumb joints slowly. Adjust the position of your lips until the sound is full and mournful. Release outer fingers to change notes.

## 5.

If you hear a loon, return the loon call. The loon may "talk" back, and may come closer to investigate. Then you'll be able to see what movements the loon makes to create its call.

# SWEEP-NETTING FOR MEADOW BUGS

**B**y the beginning of July, long-grass country is abuzz with bugs. It's amazing how many different kinds of bugs are out there. Here's a net you can make to sweep a meadow and check out the local bugs.

| You'll need: |
| --- |
| a coil of strong wire or a coat hanger |
| a tape measure |
| wire cutters |
| a penknife |
| a thin, rigid 10-foot stick |
| masking tape |
| a roll of thinner wire |
| an old pillowcase |
| scissors |
| a needle |
| thread |
| pliers |

**1.**
Snip off one yard of the strong wire with wire cutters. Bend it to make one large loop. Measure about six inches from each end of the loop and bend each end out sharply to form two prongs. (With an adult's help, a coat hanger can be made into the same shape and size.)

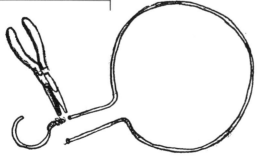

**2.**
With the penknife, carefully cut two thin ridges into opposite sides of the stick, six inches down from the top. Hold the prongs of the wire loop in place just above the ridge and secure with masking tape.

**3.**
Hold one end of the thinner wire with your thumb on the stick below the prongs. Then wind the wire up tightly around the prongs, until you get to the top of the stick.

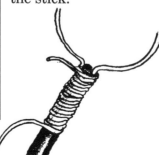

**4.**
Cut the wire, leaving a tab of a few inches of wire sticking out the end. Jab that tab and the one held down with your thumb under a couple of the wire coils.

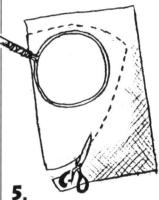

**5.**
Turn a pillowcase inside out and spread flat. Place the loop on it about two inches from the opening and touching one adjacent side. Cut a triangular shape from the pillow case, the base of the triangle being wider than the diameter of the loop and the sides tapering to a rounded bottom. Use one double fold of the pillow case as a side of the triangle.

**6.**

Sew one open side with small stitches. Turn the case right-side out so the stitching can't be seen.

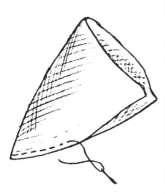

**7.**

Pull the top of the pillowcase net through the wire loop and fold the cloth back over the rim. Roll the outer edge of the cloth under again to form a hem and stitch the net into place.

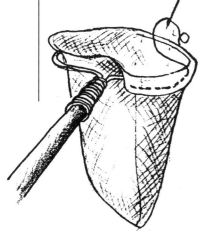

# HOW TO SWEEP-NET

On a sunny afternoon, head for a meadow with the net and a shoe box. Start anywhere in the meadow. Leaving the box on the ground, hold the net at plant height and brush quickly up and down and around the field. When you've circled back to the box, carefully shake the net into it, turning the net inside out to release all the clingers. See if you have any of the insects listed here.

When you've finished looking at the bugs, turn the box on its side and let them hop back into the meadow.

The treehopper is a tiny bug that looks like a thorn.

Katydids are all-green grasshoppers with huge, long feelers.

The black field cricket is a strange musician—it sings by rubbing its wing casings together and hears with an ear in its front leg.

The green stink bug is true to its name—as you'll find out if you disturb it.

The yellow ambushbug hides in goldenrod flowers where it really does ambush and eat flies and bees that land nearby.

The bee assassin stabs honeybees in the back with its beak while they feed.

The praying mantis looks as if it's praying, but it's really preying.

Look for the beautiful large black and yellow (argiope) garden spider.

## SPIDER **POWER**

Scientists believe the dry silk made by the orb-weaving spider may be the strongest fiber on earth. They are investigating reproducing it to make bullet-proof vests, armored vehicles, and boat hulls.

Take care not to damage spider webs. Spiders eat their old webs to help make the silk for spinning new ones.

# RAISE A MONARCH BUTTERFLY

In a summer meadow with milkweed plants, look for a monarch caterpillar. It has narrow black, yellow, and white stripes. Check an insect guide to be sure of its identity. If you have a couple of weeks to care for it, here's how to witness the remarkable change from monarch caterpillar to butterfly.

| You'll need: |
| --- |
| a large glass jar and waxed paper |
| milkweed leaves |
| a rubber band |
| a fork |
| an insect field guide |

**1.**

See page 90 for a description of milkweed. Look nearby for a caterpillar about as big as your little finger. Collect the caterpillar and the top of its plant in the glass jar. Put in a few extra milkweed leaves. Cover the jar with waxed paper and secure it with a rubber band. Punch small air holes in the waxed paper with a fork.

**2.**

Place the bottle outside where it's sheltered from direct sunlight and from rain (but not where it's damp, such as under a cabin or deck).

**3.**

Watch—but don't move—the bottle. After a few days, the caterpillar will stop moving and hang under the lid or a leaf. The caterpillar is now spinning its green case, called a chrysalis.

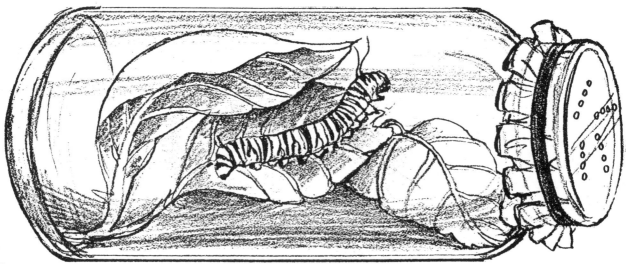

**4.**

When the chrysalis is still and green from top to bottom, take the cover off the jar and gently ease the milkweed partway out so the chrysalis is in the open air. Check every morning and count its golden spots. Before long, the chrysalis will lose its beautiful green color and turn dull and dark. When that happens, it's not dying; it's changing again. Start visiting more often.

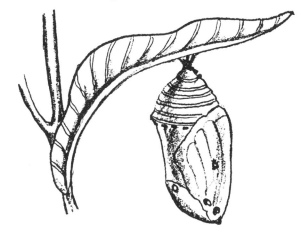

**5.**

When the chrysalis eventually turns clear, with black and orange showing through, stay nearby. The butterfly inside will soon crack the chrysalis. Then the wings will emerge, followed by the whole butterfly. Let it take its time to stretch and dry before it flops away. Look carefully to see what's happened to the golden spots.

# MONARCH MIGRATION

Monarch butterflies migrate south for the winter, just as birds do. In the autumn, they fly to Southern California and Mexico, where they hang on trees by the millions and doze through the winter. In the spring, the females fly north until they are exhausted, lay eggs before they die, and are replaced by a new generation that travels on. This happens many times before a single monarch is seen in the northern states in the summer. It may be the great-great-grandchild of one that left for last year's trip south.

79

# SUMMER BIRD FEEDERS

Hanging bird feeders is a good way to see birds up close. Here are three summer bird feeders that are easy to make. See how many different kinds of birds are attracted to the feeders.

## SEED FEEDER

**You'll need:**

| |
|---|
| a clean cardboard milk or juice carton |
| scissors |
| string |
| birdseed |

**1.**
Punch a hole in the center of the front of the milk carton with scissors and cut out the two sides and the top of a square.

**2.**
Bend the cut piece out at the bottom and snip it off, leaving a short flap for a perch. Repeat for the opposite side of the carton.

**3.**
Make a hole through the top of the milk carton with the scissors and thread string through it.

**4.**
Fill the carton with birdseed and hang the feeder from a tree limb where it can be easily seen. Make sure it's well off the ground but can still be reached for refilling. Look for seed-eaters, such as rose-breasted grosbeaks and purple finches, at the summer seed feeder.

# FRUIT FEEDER

**You'll need:**

| |
|---|
| a hammer |
| a strong nail |
| a piece of partly eaten or spoiled fruit (peach, apple, plum) |

**1.**
Hammer the nail into the side of a tree, above eye level, in a sunny spot that can be easily seen. Hammer it partway in so the nail is stuck but still stands out from the tree.

**2.**
Punch a piece of fruit onto the nail so it won't fall off.

**3.**
In the summer's heat, the fruit will start to rot and collect fruitflies. Some birds will come to eat the flies buzzing around the fruit. Others will pick at the fruit itself. When you find another piece of spoiled fruit, jab it onto the nail, too. Look for northern orioles and warblers at your fruit (and fly) feeder.

## BIRD FEEDERS AT NIGHT

Don't forget to check all the feeders at night. There may be flying squirrels, luna moths, raccoons, whippoorwills and other nocturnal creatures helping themselves.

# NECTAR FEEDER

**You'll need:**

| |
|---|
| red ribbon |
| a clear, long, thin bottle without a lid (an empty medicine bottle works well) |
| ¼ cup sugar |
| 1 cup hot tap water |
| red food coloring (optional) |
| twist tie |

**1.**
Tie the red ribbon around the neck of the bottle. (Hummingbirds are attracted to the color red.)

**2.**
Add the sugar to the water. Stir to dissolve and let the mixture cool.

**3.**
Pour the sugar and water nectar into the bottle. Add red food coloring to the water if desired. (Leftover nectar can be kept covered in the fridge for refills.)

**4.**
With the twist tie, wire the bottle to the top of a strong plant or shrub in a sunny, visible spot. If there is a patch of red, orange, or pink flowers, wire the feeder near it. Look for ruby-throated hummingbirds hovering at the nectar feeder in the eastern U.S. and rufous hummingbirds in the western U.S.

# BIRDBATH

## HUMMINGBIRD BATH

The hummingbird feeder on page 81 will attract these fascinating birds. See if they'll drop in for a bath too. Use the largest carrot or parsnip you can find.

**You'll need:**

- a penknife
- a large carrot or parsnip
- a vegetable peeler
- a hammer
- a thin nail
- a toothpick
- plastic thread or fine string
- water

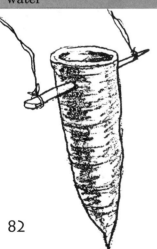

**1.**
Cut off two inches from the fat end of a carrot. Hollow out the cut end as far down as possible using the end of the peeler and a penknife.

**2.**
Gently make a small hole in each side of the carrot with the hammer and nail. Slide the toothpick through the holes, creating a perch.

**3.**
Tie a piece of thread to each end of the toothpick.

**4.**
Tie the tiny bath to the branch of a tree, preferably beside a hummingbird feeder.

**5.**
Fill the carrot regularly with water. Watch and wait for the buzzing thank-you from the hummingbird.

# GARBAGE LID

An old garbage can lid is the right depth to attract larger birds such as sparrows and robins. A metal lid can be painted brown or green or left just as is. Choose a location that is away from paths but close enough to see any bird bathers.

**You'll need:**

- a garbage can lid
- sand, dirt, or an old tire
- bricks or large stones

**1.**
Place the lid on either sand, loose dirt, or an old tire. Adjust it so it's level.

# BATH

**2.**

Surround the lid with beach stones or old bricks. They will keep the bath in place and provide landing perches for the birds.

**3.**

Fill the lid daily with fresh water. Rinse it out with a hose once a week to keep the tin from getting slimy.

# THE WATERING HOLE

This bottle bath is mounted on a deck or fence to attract passersby such as swallows, martins, meadowlarks, and bluebirds.

| You'll need: |
| --- |
| a large soda bottle |
| a piece of two-by-four slightly taller than the bottle and a pencil |
| water |
| a hammer |
| 4 nails (1 inch long) |
| 6 large rubber bands |
| a fence or deck post |
| a large margarine or yogurt tub |

**1.**

Lay the bottle on the wide side of the two-by-four. With a pencil, mark one and a half inches down from the top of the bottle and again around the fattest part. Do the same on the other side.

**2.**

Hammer the four nails into these marks part way, leaving three-fourths inch of nail sticking out.

**3.**

Knot two sets of three rubber bands together.

**4.**

Check with an adult first and then nail the two-by-four to a fence or post.

**5.**

Fill the margarine tub with a cup of water and place it on top of the post. Fill the soda bottle with water and hold a hand over the top. Invert the filled bottle into the tub. Attach it to the two-by-four by looping each knotted rubber band set around the nail on one side, across the bottle and around the nail on the other side.

**6.**

To refill, remove and fill the bottle. Add more water to the tub too. Rinse out the bottle and the tub once a week to keep the water clean.

# BUILD A BIRDHOUSE

**J**ust as different kinds of birds look different, they favor different nests and nesting sites. Here's an easy birdhouse to make that will suit a bluebird, a tree swallow, a flicker, or a house wren.

| You'll need: |
| --- |
| a large plastic vinegar or bleach bottle (half as big for wrens) and small stones |
| water and gravel |
| a sharp knife and coarse sandpaper |
| a hamer and nail |
| brown exterior latex house paint and a paintbrush |
| length of wire |
| an adult helper |

## 1.

Wash out the plastic bottle thoroughly. Add gravel to the water to make it muddy, and swirl it around inside the bottle and pour it out again. This will take away the chemical smell and leave a rougher, more natural surface on the inside.

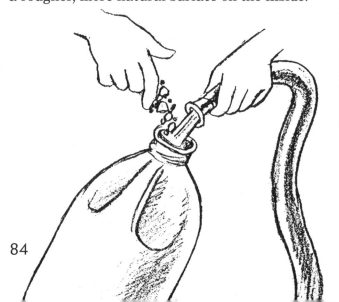

## 2.

Put the cap on the bottle and turn it upside down. Ask an adult to help cut a circular hole on one side well above the neck of the bottle, using the knife. The hole size determines the kind of birds the house will attract (see page 85).

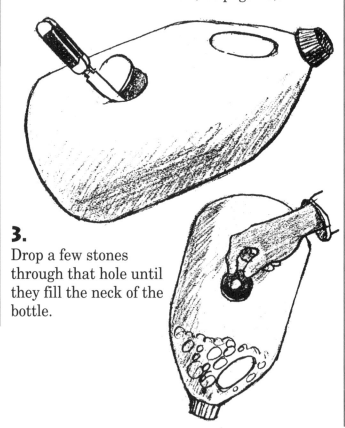

## 3.

Drop a few stones through that hole until they fill the neck of the bottle.

**4.**
Make two level holes with a hammer and nail on the sides above the entrance hole.

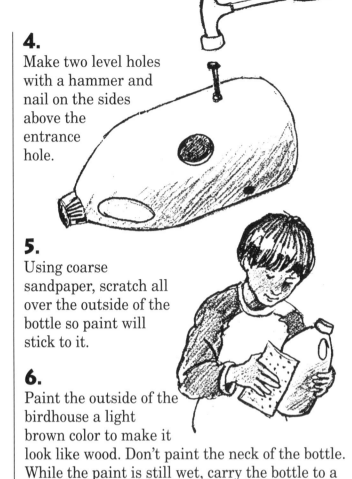

**5.**
Using coarse sandpaper, scratch all over the outside of the bottle so paint will stick to it.

**6.**
Paint the outside of the birdhouse a light brown color to make it look like wood. Don't paint the neck of the bottle. While the paint is still wet, carry the bottle to a wooded area and roll it in leaves and twigs until some have stuck to the paint.

**7.**
When the paint is dry, run wire through the air holes. Use the wire to strap the birdhouse to a tree or post at the apporpriate height for the chosen bird (see the list below). Remove the cap for drainage.

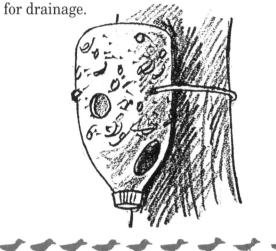

## BIRDHOUSE FACTS

| Kind of Bird | Hole Size | Nesting Location |
|---|---|---|
| bluebird | $1\frac{1}{2}$ inches | about 5 feet off the ground on a post in open country about 32 feet from a tree |
| tree swallow | 2 inches | a little higher off the ground than for a bluebird and near a pond |
| flicker | 3 inches | about 16 feet up a tree trunk on a woodland edge |
| house wren | 1 inch | on the trunk of a thick shrub about 3 feet off the ground; house wrens like two houses, one for the young, one for extra nesting materials |

# PURPLE MARTIN APARTMENT HOUSE

With the help of an adult, you can construct a purple martin apartment house.

**1.**

As described on pages 84–85, wash six or more plastic bottles and make two air holes in each. Screw on the caps.

**2.**

Ask an adult to help cut a two-inch entrance hole in each unit.

**3.**

Don't drop stones into the neck. Instead, make a few small nail holes in the bottom of the bottle so any rainwater will drain away.

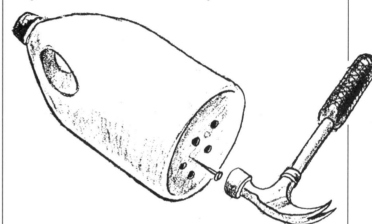

**4.**

Thread wire through the air holes and hang the apartments in threes along a wooden bar.

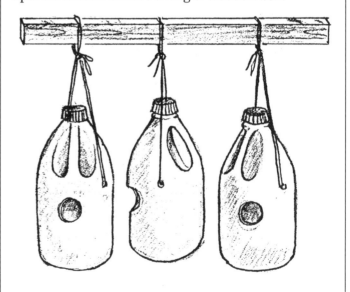

## NATURE BREAK

In 1884 a man counted the number of times adult martins in a colony visited their young with food in one day. He counted 3277 visits. When purple martins move into the apartment house, see if you get bothered by mosquitoes while sitting outside in the evening. People who live near martins often say they are never bothered by bugs—the martins have eaten them all.

**5.**

With an adult helper, nail the wooden bars on top of a pole at a height of at least ten feet—up to twenty-five feet.

Purple martins are attracted to open yards away from trees and buildings but near a pond or lake, so they can feast on insects such as mosquitoes. Set up the apartment house late in the summer and a busy colony of families may be there next summer. Pioneers believed that sprinkling broken eggshells under a martin house made it more likely to be chosen by a colony.

# COUNTING SNAKES

**C**ounting snakes can be fun. How many different kinds can you count? How many of each kind? These observations and totals can help scientists doing research.

Scientists collect data about the numbers of snakes sighted over a large region and compile an atlas incorporating the results. They keep records of snake sightings and evidence of a snake's presence—such as a shedded skin or bodily remains. By comparing the data from year to year, they can determine which kinds of snakes are thriving, which ones are in danger, and where endangered snakes have been seen so they can be protected.

If you want to help contribute to a snake atlas, count all the snakes you see over the summer. At each sighting, note its kind, the place where it was seen, the time of day, and any other details you notice. Then, send the information to the scientists who collect details about sightings from all over the state to compile their snake atlas. If you desire, you can also help track frogs, toads, turtles, birds, mammals, or plants. Here is how to become an atlaser:

**1.**
Go to the library and get a field guide to help identify different kinds of snakes. Be sure you can recognize dangerous snakes.

**2.**
Find out who's compiling the atlas on snakes in the area. Try the local naturalists' club or natural history museum.

**3.**
Make several cards like this:

My Name: _____

Address: _____

Date of Sighting: _____

Exact Location: _____

Type of Snake: _____

Weather / Time of Day: _____

Habitat: _____

What the Snake Was Doing: _____

**4.**

Every time you spot a snake, fill out a card.

**5.**

At the end of the summer, mail all the cards to the snake atlas compilers. Ask them to add the records to the state atlas.

IF YOU SEE A RATTLESNAKE OR OTHER POISONOUS SNAKE, STAY AWAY FROM IT.

## S N A K E   F A C T S

- Most mammals and birds are born in springtime, but snakelets emerge well into the summer. Many snakes lay eggs, but the garter snake and the water snake give birth to live young.

- One female garter snake usually gives birth to about twenty snakelets, but the record is eighty-seven. The young are more than five inches long at birth. A Canadian water snake may give birth to thirty to forty live snakelets, and American varieties can produce up to a hundred.

- The northern water snake can grow to be one yard long. It may look dangerous and hungry swimming across the waterfront, but it'll swim away if you clap or splash. However, big ones will give a nasty bite if you grab at them and try to pick them up.

- As a snake grows, it sheds its outer skin and replaces it with a new one. Look for the leftover skin caught between logs or rocks. A snake works its old skin off, starting at the lips, and leaves it behind all in one piece—but inside out. The shed skin is see-through, with no color, but you can make out the pattern of the scales and even the eyeballs.

- When a snake sticks its tongue out, it's not being threatening. Snakes smell with their forked tongue as well as with their nostrils. But poisonous snakes often coil and make a warning buzz or rattle that means "Watch out!"

# GARDEN GONE WILD

**Y**ou can attract some wildlife by creating a wild garden. Collect and sow seeds or transplant a few plants to create a garden full of interesting flowers. You'll have fun watching what comes to eat and visit the garden.

Select a garden spot with an adult's help. It should be away from trees, sunny, and fairly flat. A perfect place is one where grasses and weeds already grow.

In late summer, explore the area. Take along small, dry containers such as yogurt tubs. Look for plants that have gone to seed, which means they've finished flowering and are ripening seeds for next year's flowers. Collect a variety of plants and put each type in its own labeled container. A field guide to wild plants will help you identify what you collect. See Ecowatch on page 93.

Here are some seed-producing plants that are easy to find and collect.

## COLLECTING

### MILKWEED
Milkweed starts out the summer with pinkish purple flowers, then develops a broccoli-like fruiting body, followed by a seedpod bursting with white fluffy parachutes. If you want to attract monarch butterflies or monarch beetles to the wild garden, collect the brown seeds attached to the end of the parachutes.

# SEEDS

### HOLLYHOCK

Hollyhock attracts bees, hummingbirds, even moths. The seeds ripen in late August in a pod that looks like a dried fig. Many seeds are packed inside a tight circular ring. When they're very dry, they can be flicked out of the ring for planting.

### QUEEN ANNE'S LACE

Queen Anne's lace, or wild carrot, attracts beetles, such as ladybugs. The seeds can be collected at the end of the summer. The flower rolls itself up into a dry ball that looks like a small bird's nest. Collect the entire "nest."

### SUNFLOWER

In the fall, the ripe middle of the sunflower becomes a dinner plate, attracting blue jays, cardinals, orioles, chipmunks, squirrels, rabbits, and raccoons. Check around a bird feeder for a sunflower seed if you can't find a plant growing in the wild.

# PREPARING YOUR SEEDS

The seeds of most wild northern plants dry out and freeze before they start to grow in the spring. So you'll have to simulate both an autumn and winter spent in the ground to get the seeds ready for planting.
Here's how:

**1.**
Place each variety of seed on a separate sheet of newspaper to dry in the sun.

**2.**
Store the seeds inside in yogurt cups until late August.

**3.**
Place each seed variety in its own labeled jar and cover with a handful of slightly damp peat moss. Screw the lids on tightly.

**4.**
Place the jars in a shed or pump house—anywhere that's cool and out of the way. The seeds will hibernate and be ready to plant in early spring.

MORE

# SPRING PLANTING

In late May or in June, get the seed jars (see page 91) and plant the wild garden.

**1.**
Check with an adult, then prepare a soil mound for each variety of seeds. With a shovel, remove the grass from an area twenty inches in diameter. Turn the soil over and break it up with the back of the shovel. If you have any compost, now is the time to dig it in. Compost will loosen the soil and add nourishment. (See page 56 for more planting hints.)

**2.**

Leave at least one yard between each mound.

**3.**

Using a stick, poke holes four inches deep in the mound, four inches apart. Drop a seed into each hole and cover it with soil.

**4.**

Water the seeds gently and thoroughly.

## EC🔍WATCH

Collect only as many seeds as you need for the wild garden. Ten or twelve seeds of each variety should be enough. You don't want to cause a local extinction: never take all the seeds from a patch of wildflowers so the patch can keep growing next year, too. Always ask permission before collecting seeds from private property. Never take seeds or pick plants from a park or a protected area. Don't buy packs of mixed wild seeds. They often contain seeds of plants that are not local to the area and can overrun the native plants.

## A BEAUTIFUL KILLER

Purple loosestrife is a beautiful killer. It's not a native plant and it has no natural enemies. Not one North American animal feeds on its leaves, stems, or roots. Purple loosestrife is taking over wetlands and waterways, endangering the native plants. Once the native plants are gone, the local wildlife leaves or starves. Each plant can produce up to 2.7 million seeds in just one year, so it spreads like wildfire. Don't plant it in the wild garden. Here's how to identify purple loosestrife: purple or pink flower spikes that bloom from June to September; a woody, square stalk that stands from three to seven feet high with smooth-edged leaves attached directly to the stalk.

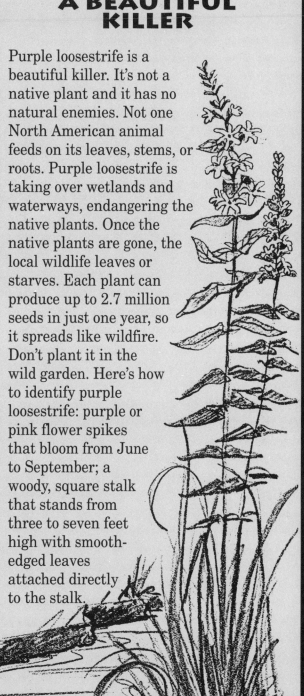

# SPYING ON AN ANTHILL

**T**he next time you leave a picnic lunch on the ground and return to find a sandwich being carried off by little black ants, follow the food back to the anthill. Construct an anthill to get an inside look at the busy lives of ants.

| You'll need: |
| --- |
| a large clear plastic soda bottle |
| a handsaw |
| a rectangular-shaped rock, a bit smaller than the bottle |
| plastic wrap |
| tape |
| a tray |
| a trowel or large spoon |
| a plastic bag |
| a pail |
| a piece of paper |
| a small piece of wet sponge |
| a cotton ball |
| a small piece of fine fabric |
| a rubber band |
| an old towel |

**1.**
Ask an adult to help cut the bottom off the plastic soda bottle, using the saw.

**2.**
Turn the bottle upside down and put the rock inside the bottle as shown. The rock will fill the center of the bottle and force the ants to construct their nests and tunnels against the walls so that you can see them working.

**3.**
Stretch plastic wrap over the bottom opening and tape it there so it forms a complete seal.

**4.**
Place the center of the tray face down on top of the bottom of the bottle. Holding the neck of the bottle with one hand and pushing down on the bottom of the tray with the other hand, turn the bottle right-side up so that it is sitting in the middle of the tray.

**5.**
Carry the trowel, plastic bag, and pail to a nearby anthill.

**6.**
Cut deep into the top of the hill with your trowel. Gently catch some of the scurrying ants in the plastic bag. Search for ants carrying cocoons—they look like pieces of dry rice. Look for a queen ant, too—she'll have a much larger body than regular worker ants.

When you've collected about twenty ants, tie the top of the bag shut. Collect some of the earth from the anthill in the pail. There needs to be enough to fill more than half of the soda bottle.

**7.**
Return to the soda bottle. Make a funnel with the piece of paper and pour the earth into the bottle so it falls around the rock.

**8.**
Poke the piece of wet sponge into the bottle neck and down onto the top of the earth.

**9.**
Drop in some crumbs from the picnic for food.

**10.**
Pour in the ants from the bag and then quickly wedge a cotton ball in the neck.

**11.**
Cover the top of the bottle with a piece of fabric held in place with the rubber band.

**12.**
Drape the towel over the bottle and leave it in the dark.

**13.**
Once a day, take off the towel, open the top, and refresh the food supply. Add a few drops of water to the sponge. Check to see if the ants have done any construction.

**14.**
After about three days you should start to see the tunnels and rooms of an anthill. You should be able to see where they take their food and how they tend their young.

**15.**
After a couple of weeks of spying on the ants, carry the tray back to the original anthill and rip the plastic off the bottom of the bottle. Let the ants return to their original home—and to their hard work, including picnic-looting.

## ANT FOOD

Ants certainly like picnics. Find out which kinds of food they prefer. Try giving the ants a small bit of cereal, a shredded piece of meat, a few seeds of grass, a few grains of sugar, and so on. Which do they gobble up first?

# ANIMAL CLUES

**Y**ou don't have to see an animal to know that it has visited the area. Animals leave clues behind that clearly say, "I've been here." So become a detective and discover who has recently visited.

### RACCOON

Overturned garbage, pilfered compost, and crayfish remains on the beach all indicate that the masked bandit has dined nearby. Raccoon paw prints look like tiny human hands.

### SKUNK

If your nose doesn't tell you, the lawn can. Holes and rolled-up grass show where the skunk's sharp claws have scrounged a meal of grubs and insects.

### DEER

Look for flattened grass in meadows or woodland clearings. Check under apple trees, too—deer love apples for breakfast.

### SQUIRREL

A log pile is a good hideout for a squirrel, mouse, or chipmunk. If you find pinecones that have been eaten clean, you have had a guest.

# PLASTER-CAST ANIMAL TRACKS

You can make a "negative" impression plaster cast of a bird or animal track. They make impressive doorstops or paper-weights.

**You'll need:**

| |
|---|
| a 2-by-8-inch piece of heavy cardboard |
| a paper clip |
| about a cup of water |
| a margarine tub |
| wall plaster |
| a stick |

**1.**
Find a clear animal or bird track in mud or sand.

**2.**
Form the cardboard into a circle, securing it with a paper clip. Place the cardboard around the track and push it gently into the soil or sand.

**3.**
Pour the water into the margarine tub, filling the cardboard mold halfway. Add the plaster to the water in the tub a little at a time, stirring with a stick until smooth. The mixture should be as thick as pancake batter. It should pour but not be too runny.

**4.**
Pour the plaster into the mold.

**5.**
Let it set for several hours until it's very hard. Drying time depends on the thickness of the cast and the dampness in the air.

**6.**
Pick up the mold and remove the cast from the ground. Dust off any loose dirt.

**7.**
Paint the track or leave it white.

97

# FLY A KITE

**T**here's nothing like the feel of a kite pulling up and away on a windy day. Have a kite ready when steady breezes blow.

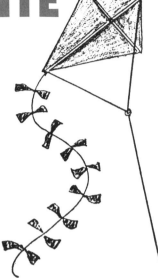

| You'll need: |
| --- |
| a felt-tip pen |
| a tape measure |
| 2 straight sticks or dowelling, about $1/4$ inch thick and about 28 inches long |
| a 3-foot fishing line |
| a 130-foot strong, thin nylon cord |
| 4 straight pins |
| a 32-inch square of light cotton |
| scissors |
| white glue |
| colored tissue paper |
| a metal soda can opening tab |
| a flat wooden stick about 6 inches long, sanded |

**1.**
Start by making the frame. With a felt-tip pen, mark a point eight inches from the end of one stick and another fourteen inches from the end of the other stick. Form a cross with the two sticks so they meet at the two marks. Wind the fishing line crosswise around the joint and knot securely.

**2.**
Cut off about fifteen feet of the nylon cord. Pin one end of the cord into the bottom tip of the frame. Stretch the cord around the frame and pin it at the other three tips. Bring it back to the bottom and secure it with the first pin. Leave the remaining cord attached to form the kite tail.

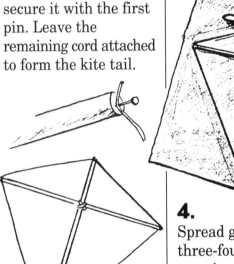

**3.**
Lay the frame on the fabric and cut out the shape of the frame. Leave an extra three-fourths inch of material all around. Snip little V's out of each point of the shape.

**4.**
Spread glue over the three-fourths-inch margin and then fold and press it back over the frame.

## 5.

To finish the tail, cut the tissue paper into twelve by six inch strips. Fold the strips in half lengthwise. Tie the middle of the strips to the tail string, spacing them about six inches apart.

## 6.

Now string the kite. Cut forty-seven inches of cord, fold it in half, push the loop end through the soda can ring, and then slip the loose ends back through the loop. Open up the cord and tie one end to the top of the kite spine and the other to the bottom.

## 7.

Tie one end of the remaining nylon cord to the flat wooden stick. Wind the cord around and around until you come to the other end. Tie that to the soda can ring. Now the kite is attached to its line and ready to fly.

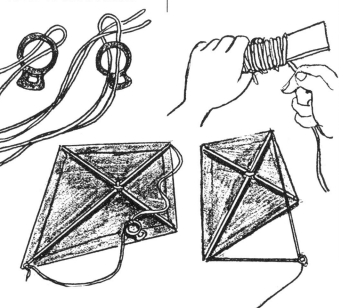

# TIPS FOR SUCCESSFUL KITE FLYING

Choose a clear day with a steady wind to try out the kite. Gusty days are hard for beginners. Stand in a place where the wind will blow the kite away from any electrical wires or kite-eating trees.

Let out several feet of the kite line. Ask a friend to toss the kite high in the air while you run the other way, into the wind, letting out line as you go.

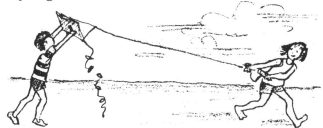

If the kite nose-dives, add cord to lengthen the tail. If it falls backward, shorten the tail.

On a calm day, try flying the kite from a motorboat.

**NEVER FLY A KITE DURING A THUNDER STORM!**

Remember, never fly kites near power lines because you could be electrocuted.

## CRAZY KITES

Before you glue on the swatch of light cotton fabric, try painting animal faces or insect bodies on it. The kite could look like a snarling cat, a lovely butterfly, or a monster mosquito.

# JUGGLE BUBBLES

**M**ost bubbles burst when touched. Using the bubble mixture below, it's possible to make bubbles that last a little longer with careful handling. It's best to do this outside, unless you like mopping floors.

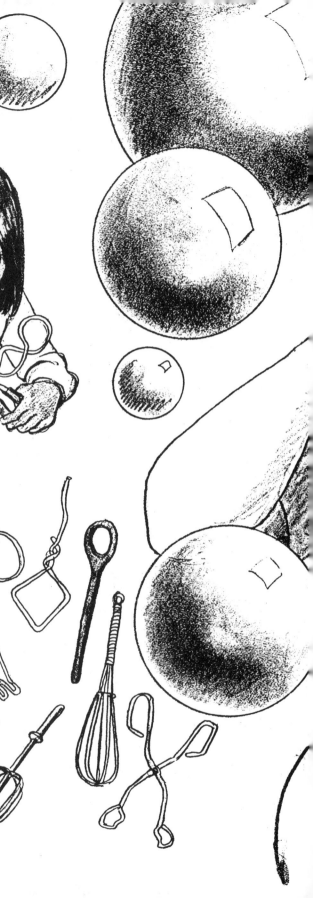

## BUBBLE SOLUTION

**You'll need:**

1/4 cup of dish detergent

3/4 cup of cold water

5 drops of glycerin (available at drugstores)

Bubbles burst because the water in the bubble solution evaporates in the air and the bubbles dry out—*pop*. The glycerin in this mixture slows down that process, helping the bubbles last longer.

## BUBBLE BLOWERS

Make bubble blowers using wire and pliers. A thin coat hanger easily bends into a small circle with a handle. Make other shapes—diamonds, figure eights, and squares. Some kitchen utensils are ready-made bubble blowers. Try a potato masher, plastic bottle cap, slotted spoon, apple corer, plastic straw . . .

## JUGGLE YOUR BUBBLES

Pull on a pair of cotton or woolen mittens or gloves. Dip the blower into the solution, blow a bubble, and with a cupped palm, bounce the bubble into the air. See how many times you can touch it before it goes *poof*.

101

# TREE FORT

If you build a tree fort this summer, you'll have a spot to call your own. You'll enjoy sharing it with a friend or with a book.

Think about the location of the tree fort. You'll want to be close enough to hear the call for dinner, but far enough to feel private. Look for a tree with lower branches about five feet from the ground. It's difficult and dangerous to build too high in the tree. One solid, sturdy tree or a clump of smaller trees growing close together will support the hideout.

Once you've picked a location, become an architect and design the fort. Then, change hats and become a carpenter and build it. Make sure to check with an adult before starting to build.

| You'll need: |
| --- |
| a measuring tape |
| a pencil and paper |
| a ladder |
| scrap wood |
| a handsaw |
| a hammer |
| 2-inch nails |
| 4-inch nails |
| a drill |
| an adult helper |

**1.**
Climb the tree to the first main branches, carrying a measuring tape, pencil, and paper. (Use a ladder if necessary, with the help of an adult.)

**2.**
Measure the distance between the branches.

**3.**
Sketch a rough layout of the floor plan. It is possible that a triangular or quadrilateral shape will fit neatly on top of the lower branches. You can adjust the floor later if it's uneven.

**4.**
You'll need wood: two-by-fours for the frame and the railings, and a sheet of plywood or planks for the floorboards and railings.

**5.**
The frame pieces should extend beyond the tree trunk. It is better to cut the pieces too long and trim them later than to cut them too short. Using the sketch as a guide, measure the two-by-four and mark with a pencil.

**6.**
Ask an adult to help saw three or four pieces to form the frame for the floor. Nail them together using two-inch nails.

**7.**
The adult helper will have to help hoist the frame up into the tree. Avoid pruning or cutting off branches—they provide more privacy.

**8.**
If the floor frame is not level, slide an extra piece of wood under the side that is too low.

**9.**
Hammer the frame securely into the tree, using four-inch nails.

MORE

103

## 10.

If you're using planks for the floorboards, use the sketch and the measuring tape to determine how many boards are required and what length they should be. Not all the floorboards need to be the same length. Plan ahead so you don't waste wood. Use the measuring tape and pencil to mark the planks.

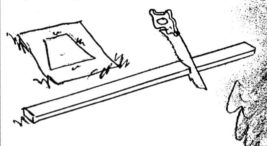

## 11.

Saw the planks to the measured length. Lay them across the frame, leaving a small gap between each board for drainage. Nail the floorboards onto the frame, using two-inch nails.

## 12.

If you have a piece of plywood, use a pencil and ruler to draw the dimensions of the frame on the wood. Using a saw, cut the plywood to size. Using a drill or a large nail and hammer, make drainage holes in the floor. Lay the board across the frame and nail it in place, using two-inch nails.

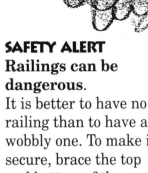

**SAFETY ALERT**
**Railings can be dangerous**.
It is better to have no railing than to have a wobbly one. To make it secure, brace the top and bottom of the railing with pieces of two-by-four. Decide which three sides of the fort to rail in, then proceed to make the railing as follows:

## 13.
Measure two feet up from the floor of the fort. Mark the tree trunk with a pencil.

## 14.
As you did for the floor frame, measure, sketch a layout, and then cut pieces of two-by-four to form a frame for the railing. Nail them into the tree trunk at the pencil marks, using four-inch nails.

## 15.
Cut planks into two-foot lengths. Nail them on the outside of the fort to the two-by-four frame, using two-inch nails.

If the fort is too high off the ground to climb up easily, turn to page 55 and make a Tarzan rope to help you scale the tree trunk. Pull the rope up after you to control who comes into the fort.

The construction of the fort is now complete, but to add some finishing touches, turn the page.

# FORT DECOR

**H**ere are some ideas to jazz up the tree fort.

## PERSONALIZED SIGN

Give the fort a name and post it on a sign.

| You'll need: |
| --- |
| a permanent marker or outdoor paint |
| a 12-by-6 inch plywood board |
| a hammer |
| 2-inch nails |
| an adult helper |

**1.**
Choose a name for the fort. It can include your own name, such as Robbie's Roost or Ellen's Aerie. Or simply write "Kids Only" or "Private Property."

**2.**
Write or paint the name of the tree fort on the board.

**3.**
Hammer the sign up near the entrance of the fort. Nail it into the wooden part of the fort, not the tree trunk.

# BASEBALL HOLDER

| You'll need: |
| --- |
| a small tin can |
| a hammer |
| 2-inch nails |

**1.**
A tuna fish or cat food can is the right size to hold a baseball. Using the hammer, smooth the edge where the lid was removed.

**2.**
Choose a spot for the holder. You'll need to nail it into a two-by-four.

**3.**
Nail the tin so that it is level. You'll always be able to find the baseball when you want to play catch.

# FIRE FIGHTER'S POLE

When it's time for dinner or there are too many mosquitoes in the fort, here's a way to make a speedy exit.

| You'll need: |
| --- |
| a shovel |
| a long piece of plumbing tube 6 inches in diameter |
| a bag of cement |
| bungee cord or cord for lashing |

**1.**
Locate the fire fighter's pole where there is a clear drop to the ground, away from tree branches and shrubs. You'll need to secure the top of the pole in a branch high up in the tree, above the fort.

**2.**
Dig a hole about one yard deep.

**3.**
Place the plumbing tube in the hole and wedge the top in branches above the fort, close to the tree trunk.

**4.**
Mix the cement according to the directions on the package. Pour it into the hole. Allow the cement to dry around the pole.

**5.**
Pack dirt on top of the cement.

**6.**
Secure the top of the pole with a bungee cord or rope by tying the pole to a branch of the tree. Ask an adult to check that the pole is stable.

107

# INTRUDER ALARMS

It's nice to know when company is calling. Rig up an alarm system for the fort so you won't be taken by surprise.

**You'll need:**

5 tin cans (soup size)

a hammer

a large nail

string

scissors

15 pebbles

**1.**
Wash the tin cans and remove the labels.

**2.**
Using a nail, hammer four holes in the lid of each can, including one in the middle for hanging up the alarm.

**3.**
Cut five 15-inch pieces of string.

**4.**
Thread a piece of string through the hole in the center of each can. Tie a knot on the inside of the can.

**5.**
For each can, cut three pebble strings six inches in length.

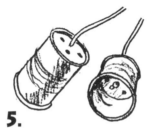

**6.**
Tie and knot each string around one pebble as you would wrap a package.

**7.**
Thread the strings with pebbles through the remaining holes, allowing the pebbles to dangle freely inside the can. Knot each string on the outside of each can.

**8.**
Tie the cans to a branch near the entrance to the fort. When the cans ring like a bell, you'll know you have a visitor.

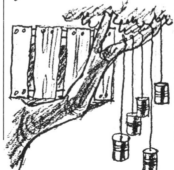

# CUBBY

A cubbyhole is a good place to store the things you want to leave in your fort, such as a penknife or a book.

**You'll need:**

a measuring tape

a one-by-six plank, about 39 inches in length

a hand saw

a hammer

2-inch nails

a pencil

**1.**
Measure, mark and then saw two 12-inch pieces of the plank. These two pieces will form the bottom and the back of the cubby.

## 2.

Measure and mark a six-inch piece on the plank. Draw a line to form a right-angle triangle as shown. Saw this piece. These two pieces will form the ends of the cubby.

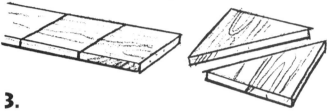

## 3.

Nail the bottom and the back of the cubby together. A nail at each end and two in between should be sufficient. Then nail the triangular ends onto the cubby.

## 4.

Choose a spot in the fort for the cubby and nail it in place.

# BIRD WATCH

In mid-August, warblers begin their fall migration. If you sit quietly in the fort, you can watch as the warblers flit through in waves. They don't flock and travel large distances in the daytime. They seem to go tree by tree, feeding and chirping along the way. A field guide to birds will help identify the warblers, but they aren't called confusing fall warblers for nothing! In fall they all have similar plumage—mostly olive green, white, and yellow. Watch carefully for the subtle differences between them—white wing bars, eye patches, or yellow throats.

# SECRET COMMUNICATIONS

**S**ometimes it's hard to find any privacy. For the times when you want to have a private conversation or send a secret message, here are two activities to show you how.

## SEND A JUICY MESSAGE

**You'll need:**

| |
|---|
| 1 stick |
| 1 tbsp lemon juice |
| an eggcup |
| paper |
| a lamp |

**1.**
Find a stick shaped like a pencil.

**2.**
Squeeze the lemon juice into the eggcup "inkwell."

**3.**
Dip the stick "pencil" into the lemon and write a message on a sheet of plain white paper. When the "ink" dries, the page will appear blank.

**4.**
To decode the message, hold the paper near a light bulb. The heat from the lamp will cook the lemon and turn it to carbon, making the message appear black.

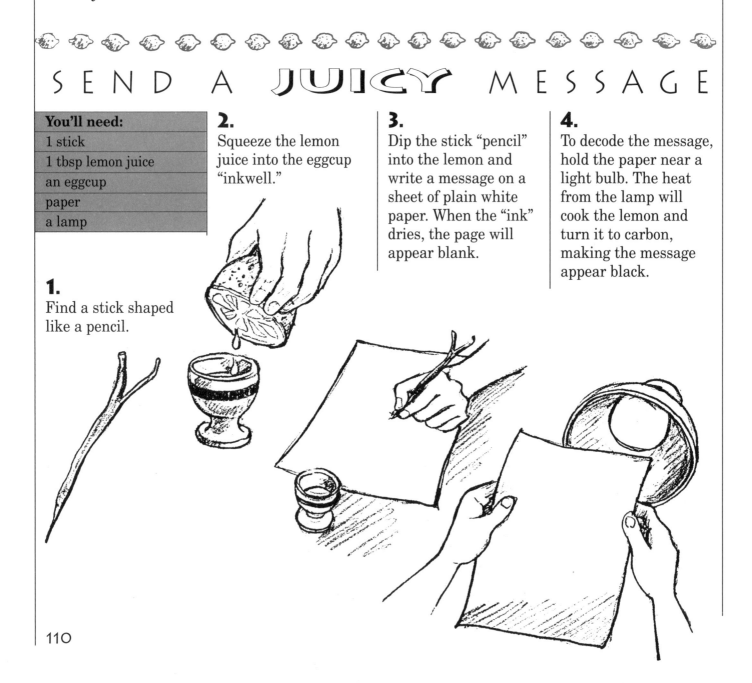

# CAN-CORD PHONE

| You'll need: |
| --- |
| a can opener |
| 2 small empty cans |
| a heavy-weight paper bag |
| a pencil |
| scissors |
| 2 rubber bands |
| petroleum jelly |
| a darning needle |
| a long piece of string |

**1.**
Remove the lids of the cans—top and bottom. If the can has sharp edges, ask an adult to help file the edges smooth.

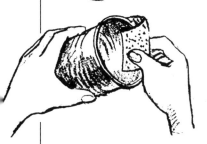

**2.**
Place your cans on the paper bag and draw circles two inches larger than each can. Cut them out, using scissors.

**3.**
Dampen the papers and wrap them over one end of each can. Hold each paper in place with rubber bands. These are the receiving ends.

**4.**
Allow the paper to dry. Now smooth a small amount of petroleum jelly on the paper. The grease will make the paper stronger.

**5.**
Thread the darning needle with the string. Pass the needle through the center of one paper "receiver." Gently make a knot on the inside. Repeat with the second phone. Now you've made the connection and the can-cord phones are ready to use.

Make sure to hold the string taut above the ground so that it does not touch anything. When you speak into the phone, both the paper and the string will vibrate. When the vibrations (or sound waves) reach the other phone, your voice will be heard in it.

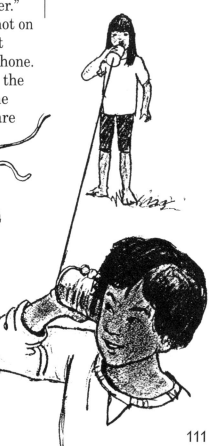

# AFTER DARK

There's lots to do outside on a summer's night. Start a bonfire and swap stories, or shut off the lights and watch a meteor shower. Prowl and get to know the nightlife by the shine in their eyes. Or learn to distinguish between frogs and toads by their night calls. Read on to find out how.

# CAMPFIRE RING

**P**eople like to have a campfire in the summer—it's sometimes cool in the evening and a fire is warm company. And how else can you roast marshmallows? First, find a good site. Then follow the directions below and have fun by the fire.

## CHOOSING A SITE

Ask an adult to help choose the location of the fire pit. It's best to place it out in the open. If there is a rocky point, that's an ideal spot. If necessary, you can build a fire pit on a lawn, but dig out the grass around it first. Dry grasses and leaves can catch fire, as can overhanging trees, lawn cuttings, bushes, and shrubs. Anything too close to the fire pit can accidentally catch fire, so choose the site carefully.

Collect large stones for marking the edge of the fire pit. Bricks can be used as an alternative. Take time to arrange the rocks neatly and adjust each one, making sure it's not wobbly. Make the fire pit a small, manageable size. The size of a bicycle wheel is big enough. Turn the page to find out how to lay the fire.

# BUILDING A FIRE

Now you're ready to lay a fire in the fire pit. If it's windy, wait for a calmer night. If it's been raining and the ground is wet, lay some bark from a dead tree on the bottom of the pit.

Now you need a wood pile, with three sizes of wood: tinder, kindling, and fuel.

## TINDER

Tinder will flare up and catch fire when lit with a match. Hunt for dead, dry pine needles, birchbark from fallen trees, and little twigs. Or make a furze stick (see the box below). Place several furze sticks on top of other tinder. (See page 150 for a description of other kinds of tinder.)

## KINDLING

Make the kindling into a teepee shape, directly over the tinder. Kindling burns longer than the "poof" ignition of tinder. Collect sticks that are at least as thick as a pencil. Dry pieces of bark work, too, but don't strip bark from a live tree. Ask an adult to light the tinder underneath the kindling using a match.

## FUEL

Once the kindling is burning well, add fuel. Fuel keeps the fire going. You'll need an adult to help gather a supply of larger logs as thick as an arm or leg. Look for fallen trees, which can be sawed up into fuel. Never cut down a live tree—use only old, dry wood.

## MAKING A FURZE STICK

To make a furze stick, you need a sharp penknife (see the next page for knife safety) and a dry stick that's about the size of a medium carrot. Hold the top of the stick firmly in one hand. With the knife blade pointing away from you, loosen little pieces from the bottom of the stick without removing them. Work up to the center of the stick, creating featherlike pieces of wood as thin as a match. Turn the stick the other way around and work to the middle again. This way your hand never comes near the blade of the knife.

## COOK IN A FIRE PIT

A cooking fire is built slightly differently from a comfort fire. Light the fire between two wet logs or large rocks set slightly apart. Rest a cooking pot on top of the logs.

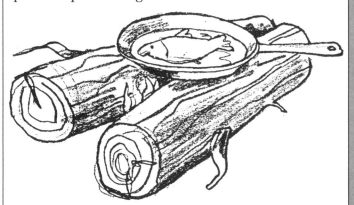

## PUTTING OUT A FIRE

Putting out a fire takes as much care as lighting one. Never leave a fire unattended. When the beans and the marshmallows are eaten, put the fire out—completely. Douse the entire fire pit with water. Stir the ashes, coals, and fuel with a long stick and pour on more water. Repeat until the fire pit is completely cold. Fire can travel underground along roots, so it's important to double-check that the soil under the fire is cold and wet.

## KNIFE **SAFETY**

A good knife and a hatchet are essential tools for lighting a fire, but it takes careful practice with an adult to learn to use them properly.

Remember, knives are tools, not toys. You won't outgrow them. So choose the tools to last. You'll need a simple folding pocketknife. Extra gadgets aren't needed. Choose a small, light hatchet.

Take care of the knife and hatchet by keeping them clean, dry, and sharp. Sharpen them on a sharpening stone by using a drop of oil, such as WD-40, on the blades and stroking the blade away from the body at a twenty-degree angle. Keep the blades lightly oiled.

Store the knife and hatchet away from younger children. Knives should be kept closed or in a sheath. Hatchets should be stored with the blade covered with a leather sheath.

# BONFIRE EVENING

It's a dark and moonless night. The bonfire's crackling and your family and friends are toasting marshmallows. The scene is set for a ghost story. Check out the caldron for the essential ingredients of a spine-tingling tale. Then put a flashlight under your chin to distort your face and make scary shadows.

QUAVERY VOICE
DRAG IT OUT. CREATE SUSPENSE
BLACK CATS, NUMBER 13, WALKING UNDER A LADDER
AWFUL NOISES—SCREAMS, MOANING, OWL HOOTS, DEEP VOICES
BLOODY AX
SKELETONS
REPETITION
GREEN HANDS, GOLDEN ARMS, BLOODY FINGERS
KNOCK ON THE DOOR
MYSTERIOUS PHONE CALLS
OLD OUTHOUSE
ABANDONED FARM
SHIPWRECK OFF THE POINT
CLAPS OF THUNDER, GUSTS OF WIND
CREAKING DOOR
BRANCHES SCRATCHING ON THE WINDOW
SHOUT OUT THE PUNCH LINE

Here's a sample ghost story you can adapt for the bonfire. Use the names of people present and describe a room in the cottage. Make everybody listening fear the story will happen to them. Be prepared to leave the light on when you go to sleep tonight!

Y ou are all alone in the cottage. The phone rings, and you answer it. A high-pitched, squeaky voice says, "I'm holding a bloody finger and I'm three doors away." The line goes dead. Your skin begins to crawl. You check all the locks on the doors and windows, draw the curtains, and listen to the rain on the roof. The phone rings again. The same hideous voice says, "I'm holding a bloody finger and I'm two doors away." Click. The refrigerator squeals to life and you jump out of your chair, hands sweating. RRRRing. "I'm holding a bloody finger and I'm one door away." Click. Your heart is pounding and you dash around wildly. A clap of thunder rocks the cottage. The lights flicker. Suddenly there is a pounding on the door. You know you shouldn't answer but some unnatural force drags you toward the door. You turn the knob, very slowly. Standing on the doorstep is little Ian from down the road. He holds up his bloody finger and says, "Do you have a bandage?"

## CAMPFIRE SINGALONG

After ghost-story telling, you may want to lighten up the mood with a singalong. A good opener is the tried-and-true "Quartermaster store" song, which you can adapt. Here are some ideas to get your imagination started:

"There were loons loons walking like raccoons on the shore on the shore, there were loons loons walking like raccoons on the hot and sandy shore." Or, "There were fleas fleas riding water skis." Or, "There were snakes snakes swimming in the lake."

Make sure to bring in all the voices around the fire and encourage everyone to make up a verse. This could become a campfire tradition.

# NIGHT-LIGHT

**T**he light outside the cottage that allows you to see at night is also ideal for attracting nocturnal, or night, creatures. So turn on the outside light and watch.

## MOTH MANIA

Late in the afternoon, in early summer, smear ripe banana or peanut butter on a tree near the light. At nightfall, sit back in the shadows and wait. Try checking the tree early in the morning to see whether any daytime creatures like bananas.

Moths prefer the dark, but they'll come to an outdoor light in search of food. Mosquitoes, mayflies, and midges will also swarm around the light and attract bigger insect predators. Even a beautiful lunar moth may visit, with its huge, smoky, pale green wings. If a lunar moth is attracted to the night-light, treat it with respect. They live just a few days—only long enough to mate and lay eggs.

## TOAD HOLES

Toads feed at night and will position themselves just beyond an outside light. Their quick tongues dart out and snare unsuspecting insects. Build the toad a permanent home so that a natural mosquito controller can move in.

| You'll need: |
| --- |
| a shovel |
| a 12-inch piece of pipe or weeping tile |
| a small pail of sand |
| a handful of gravel-size rocks |

**1.**
Situate the toad hole in the sheltered shade just outside the range of the outside light. Beside a stairway is perfect.

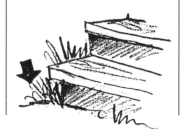

**3.**
Pour about eight inches of sand in the hole for drainage so that there won't be a puddle after it rains.

**2.**
Dig a hole at an angle about 32 inches deep and a little wider than the pipe. Put the pipe in the hole, following the angle.

**4.**
Drop in a few pebbles and stones for the toad to perch on. Check the toad hole each night to see if a toad has moved in.

## ECOWATCH

Now that you've invited a toad to move in, enjoy watching it but don't handle it. Toads don't give people warts, but they do secrete a substance through their skin that is poisonous to small predators such as weasels, foxes, and raccoons. Listen for the toad trilling. Its high, single note is softer and longer than a frog's croaking.

# BATS

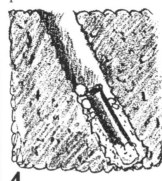

In late evening, bats begin their nocturnal activities with a drink from a lake. Then you can see them swooping near the lights, looking for prey. Listen for their high-pitched clicks, buzzes, and cries. They use the echoes of their own voices to locate prey and avoid obstacles as they fly.

Some of these sounds you can hear, others are too high-pitched for human ears. If a moth starts to fly in a zigzag pattern or dive-bombs to the ground and hides in the grass, there is a bat looking for food close by. Turn the page to find out how to build a bat hangout.

## BATS INSIDE

Bats should never be picked up. They can carry rabies and when startled, they will bite. The best way to get a bat out of a cottage is to open all the windows and doors. If this doesn't work, ask an adult to throw a light blanket over the bat and gently take it outdoors. Discourage bats from nesting inside by caulking cracks in walls and chimneys. Bats can slip through very narrow spaces.

# BUILD A BAT HANGOUT

**O**ne bat can eat five hundred mosquitoes in an hour on a summer's night. Make a bat box to make use of this remarkable and cheap insect-control service.

| You'll need: |
|---|
| a handsaw |
| a rough, unplaned, untreated plank of wood about 3/4 inch thick, 6 inches wide, and at least 16 inches long |
| a pencil |
| 4 strips of wood, each about 3/4-by-6-inches |
| white carpenter's glue |
| a hammer and nails or a screwdriver and screws |
| scrap of tarpaper (a dark green plastic garbage bag will also work) and tacks |
| an adult helper |

## 1.
Ask an adult to help saw a piece of plank about ten inches long for the backboard.

## 2.
Saw another piece at least six inches long for the frontboard. Lay the frontboard on the backboard one inch from the top and draw a pencil line on the backboard all around it.

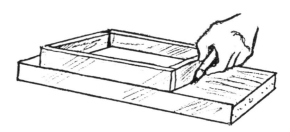

## 3.
Remove the frontboard. Lay the smaller strips of wood on their edges inside the pencil line and saw them so they fit neatly around. Trim about one and a half inches from the floor strip (see illustration) and angle it upward to make an entrance.

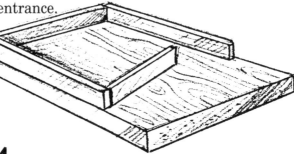

## 4.
Glue the side and top strips onto the backboard. Nail or screw them in place. Screw in the bottom strip loosely, so that it can be removed in order to clean out the bat box once a year.

**5.**

Smear glue along the edge of the top and sides of the frontboard and lay it on top of the strips. Then nail or screw the frontboard down.

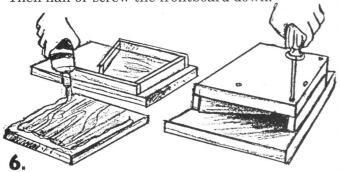

**6.**

Tack tarpaper on the back of the backboard, pull it over the top, and tack it partway down the frontboard.

**7.**

Now hang the bat box. Choose a spot sheltered from the wind, on an outside wall or on a tree but away from branches, and facing southwest or southeast so that the inside will get warm in the sun. The box is best situated near a meadow or pond, where bats can hunt mosquitoes. Nail the backboard top and bottom so the entrance is at least sixteen feet above the ground.

## BAT FACTS

- Bats may move into the bat box soon after it's hung—or wait to go house-hunting in early April. Leave the box up over the winter.
- In summer, mother bats like their nest to be toasty warm—80° to 90°F if possible. Males choose cooler hangouts, away from the young.
- Bats roost by day and fly off to feed at night. Watch the box at dusk to see them take off.
- Bats are careful about personal hygiene. They lick their fur, scratch themselves, and wipe their faces. They are particularly fussy about keeping their wings clean. Bat feces, called guano, are a great fertilizer for the garden, and will collect under the bat box.
- Most bats in the United States eat only insects. In some parts of the world, bats eat pollen and are important pollinators of fruits. Blood-sucking vampire bats are tropical.
- Bats will leave their nesting spots by September to look for warmer winter hangouts in hollow trees, caves, and the attics of old buildings. They hibernate over winter.

# NIGHT PROWL

**T**o find out what goes bump in the night, take a night prowl outside. You'll be surprised by who's making those noises out there.

| You'll need: |
|---|
| a red bandanna or scarf |
| a flashlight |
| dark clothing (be sure to stay away from roads) |
| a friend |

**1.**
On a clear night, tie the red bandanna over the flashlight so the beam is still strong but glows red.

**2.**
Put on dark clothes. Rub dirt on your face and hands, too, if you want to really blend in.

**3.**
Take a friend and tell an adult where you're going and when you'll be back. Step outside, away from the lights, and turn on the flashlight.

**4.**
Stand still to get used to the dark. Look at the trees and watch how moonlight and breezes play on them. Each kind of tree moves in its own way. Maple leaves, for instance, have a darker top than underside, so when a breeze passes, the whole tree ripples light and dark like running water.

**5.**

When you're used to the dark, walk ahead softly. Sweep the dark with the light. When you hear a sound, shine the flashlight beam in its direction.

Here are some of the things you may see and what they may be:

black, zigzagging shadows in the air — bats

flashes of light in the grass or bushes — fireflies

tiny glowing dots of light on the ground or in rotting logs — beetle grubs or fungus

tiny, crawling specks of white — wolf spider eyes

large, close-set, orange eyes — bear—careful—walk away noisily, yelling and throwing things hard on the ground

bright yellow eyes — raccoon

shining green eyes — bullfrog

bright white eyes — dog, coyote, or wolf

dull white eyes — whippoorwill

flash of white tails hopping near the ground . . . — cottontail rabbit

or bounding away above eye level — white-tailed deer

white streaks waddling along the ground — skunk

a silent shadow gliding from tree to tree — owl

# NIGHT OWL

When you hear an owl call, stop and listen for the next round. Count the number of sounds and memorize the rhythm. When you think you've got it, repeat the call several times. The owl may come to investigate, thinking another owl is trespassing on its territory.

Here are the sounds and rhythms of owl calls you may hear:

**HOOTING:**

**great horned owl**
WhaWhaWha - Whooo - Whooo
WhaWhaWhaWha - Whooo - Whooo

**barred owl**
Whoo - Whoo - WhaWho - Whoohoohoohoaw
(sounds like "Who cooks, who cooks for you all")

**SHRIEKING:**

**barn owl**
Chaaaaaaaaaaaaaaaaaaaaaaaaaak
(can hiss, too)

**long-eared owl**
Waaaaaaaaaaaaaaaaaaaaaaaaaaaaaa
(can be wheezy or shrill)

**WAILING:**

**screech owl**
Oo-o-o-o-o-o-o-o-o-000000
(descending and quavering like a faraway ghost)

125

# WORM FARM

**W**hen you're on the night prowl, look for some worms, too. Earthworms can be kept in a jar for a few weeks if you duplicate the environment in which they were living and provide them with fresh food and water. The key to success is care. In a few short weeks, you can have a snarl of tunnels to watch and—with luck—baby worms. At the end of the summer, add the worms to the composter and they will help create new soil for next summer's tomatoes.

| You'll need: |
|---|
| the largest jar you can find—a 1-gallon condiment jar works well |
| loose soil |
| sand |
| water |
| leaves |
| lettuce |
| a flashlight |
| 4 to 6 worms |
| a clean yogurt or margarine container |
| a brown paper bag |
| scissors |
| tape |

## 1.

Fill the jar three-quarters full with layers of loose garden or woodland soil and sand. Do not pack it down. Sprinkle lightly with water. Place several leaves on the top and a few bits of lettuce.

## 2.

Keep the worm farm in a cool place, such as a shed or basement. Choose a spot away from sunlight and too much heat. Now you're ready to hunt for worms.

## 3.

Worms can be easily found after rain or at night, using a flashlight. They live in cool, damp places, so look under logs, at the edges of woods, or dig in the garden. Collect four to six worms, along with a handful of soil, in the yogurt cup.

**4.**

Place the worms in their prepared home and leave them undisturbed for a few days, to let them settle in.

**5.**

Make a protective paper sleeve that will slip over the outside of the jar to keep out light and heat. It is easily made with a brown paper bag, scissors, and some tape. It should be wide enough so it can be slipped off for viewing the worms.

**6.**

Replace the lettuce leaves every other day.

**7.**

Return the worms to their original home or add them to the composter when you're finished watching the wormery.

## FOOD AND WATER

Worms will eat a variety of garden leaves, so try several kinds and note what disappears and what is left alone. Try carrot tops, cabbage, or lettuce leaves. Remove any rotting food from the jar.

Worms need water, too, but not very much. Worms breathe through the skin and will drown if the soil is too wet. Keep the soil damp by misting the inside of the jar with a squirt gun or letting a few drops drip from your finger.

# WORM-WATCHING

Now prepare for some serious worm-watching. You will be able to see their tiny, hair-like "feet," called setae, as the worms slither up the side of the jar. Are they moist and slimy? Which end is which? The mouth opens and shuts as they move along. Do they ever travel backward? Tap on the outside of the jar and see what they do. What does the soil look like after a few days? Have the worms mixed up the layers of sand and soil?

Worms are blind, but they are sensitive to light. They are nocturnal, slipping back into the soil by dawn. That helps them avoid the hunting beaks of robins. Use a flashlight to check on the worm farm at night. Do they react to the light?

Worms are also deaf, but they can perceive vibration. When they sense the approach of birds or animals, they retreat into their burrows.

# STARS IN YOUR EYES

**T**he country is a great place to stargaze. There's so much to see in the sky, and away from city lights, the stars look clearer.

Summer is the best time to see the Milky Way running northeast to southwest across the night sky. There are so many stars in the Milky Way that, in some places, they seem to smudge together. Only in the summer do the constellations Sagittarius and Scorpio peek up over the southern horizon. The biggest annual display of shooting stars, the Perseid meteor shower, happens in early August. On clear nights, you can trace satellites, watch northern lights dance, and even spot the moons of Jupiter.

Here's how to make a simple reflecting telescope to get a look at summer's star show.

| You'll need: |
| --- |
| a curved shaving mirror |
| a small flat mirror |
| a magnifying glass |

**1.**

Face the shaving mirror so it points at the moon or at star you want to see.

**2.**

Hold a flat mirror in front of it so you can see the reflection of the shaving mirror in it.

**3.**

Look into that reflection with the magnifying glass. Everything will look much closer through the magnifying lens.

The reflecting telescope reveals surprising pocks and ragged lumps on the familiar soft face of the moon.

# SHOOTING STAR WATCH

The best way to watch the Perseid meteor shower is a sleep-out on August 11, 12, or 13. These are the nights, each summer, that the earth's orbit passes through a band of space debris that was once released from a comet when it got too close to the sun. Each piece of debris is hardly bigger than a flake of dust, but when one hits the earth's atmosphere, it is transformed into the dazzling arc of light we call a meteor or shooting star—and then it disappears.

Find a cozy spot to lay the blankets where there is a view of the entire sky. Then lie back and watch—you'll see about one meteor a minute. If you wake up during the night, check the sky. There will be more shooting stars after midnight.

# SUMMER CONSTELLATIONS

## LOOKING NORTH BEFORE MIDNIGHT

- The **Big Dipper** got its name from a long-handled ladle used to scoop water from a pail in pioneer times. In England, the same star formation is called the Plough or the Wagon.

- Even though they lived thousands of miles and years apart, both North American Native people and ancient Greeks saw a bear in the stars around the Big Dipper. Nowadays, the constellation is called **Ursa Major**, the Great Bear.

- The **North Star** is positioned as if it has been poured out of the Big Dipper. If you look at the North Star, all the other stars seem to move around it, because the earth rotates with its axis directly underneath.

- The North Star forms the tip of the handle of the **Little Dipper**, also called **Ursa Minor** or the Little Bear.

- The constellation **Cassiopeia** makes a large, wobbly W at the north end of the Milky Way.

## LOOKING SOUTH BEFORE MIDNIGHT

- Some people say that **Sagittarius**, at the base of the Milky Way, looks somewhat like a teapot. To ancient Greeks, it looked like a centaur—half man, half horse.

- Next to the teapot, the constellation **Scorpius** has the giant red star called **Antares** for a head. Scorpius is so far south that its entire body appears above the horizon only on very dark, clear summer nights.

## LOOKING OVERHEAD BEFORE MIDNIGHT

- The **Summer Triangle** is easy to spot because it's made up of three of the brightest stars in the night sky—**Vega**, **Altair**, and **Deneb**.

- Vega, the brightest star in the Summer Triangle, forms the center of the constellation **Lyra**, the Harp.

- Altair, the southern star in the Summer Triangle, is the head of **Aquila**, the eagle.

- Deneb is the top end of the **Northern Cross**. The ancient Greeks saw that same formation as **Cygnus**, the swan, with Deneb as the swan's tail.

- To the west of the Summer Triangle, look for the small and beautiful constellation **Corona Borealis** or Northern Crown.

- Far to the west is the bright orange star **Arcturus**. Arcturus is at the bottom of a constellation that looks like a kite. The Greeks called the constellation **Bootes**, the Herdsman.

To find constellations in the night sky, look north and hold this book overhead with the page facing down, or look south and turn the diagram upside down.

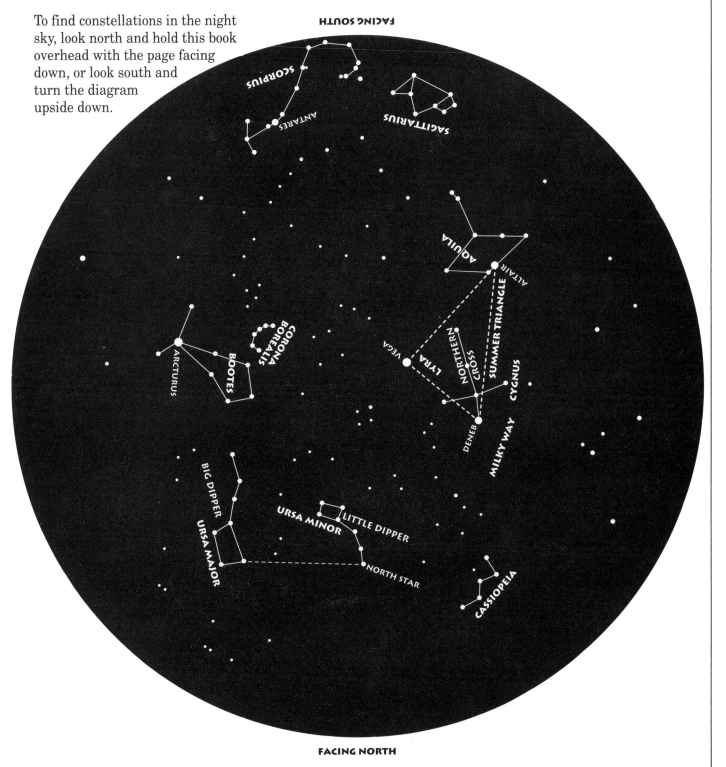

# HIKING AND CAMPING

Sometimes it's fun to get away from home base for a while. In this section, you'll learn what to bring on a hike and how to plan a cookout. You'll find out how to tell the direction you're traveling and what to do about poison ivy and mosquitoes. Maybe you'd like to develop wilderness survival skills in case you need to use them one day.

# EXPEDITION BACKPACK

**D**on't throw away those favorite old jeans. Remodel them to make a backpack. Fill the pockets with hiking essentials so you'll be ready to go when the weather is right.

| You'll need: |
| --- |
| an old belt or a piece of rope |
| a pair of old jeans |
| 2 pieces of old sheet, 4 inches by 5 feet |

**1.**
Insert the belt or rope through the belt loops of the jeans.

**2.**
Tie the bottom of each pant leg closed with one end of a piece of sheet. Knot tightly.

**3.**
Slide the other end of the sheet into the belt loops at the back of the jeans to form the straps of the backpack. Adjust the length of the sheet so the straps fit. Knot in place.

**4.**
Fill the pants with hiking gear and tighten the belt to close the top of the backpack.

**5.**
Decorate the backpack with paint, embroidery, or a collection of buttons.

## HIKING ESSENTIALS

Check out the list below for the items you should bring on a hike, then turn to Day Hike (page 136) to plan a successful hike.

1. bandages
2. a thermos and cup
3. a garbage bag
4. tissues or toilet paper
5. sunscreen
6. a hat
7. a raincoat
8. a notebook
9. a pencil
10. a yogurt tub with holes in lid
11. insect repellent
12. a penknife
13. matches

1. *Bandages*: Keep bandages clean in their box or in a plastic bag. Always wash a cut or blister with soap and dry well before bandaging.

2. *A thermos and cup*: It is important to drink enough fluids on a day hike. Streams and lakes may look clear but the water is not always safe to drink.

3. *A garbage bag*: Leave the trail as clean or cleaner than you found it. Carry out everything you carried in and pick up trash left by less thoughtful people.

4. *Tissues or toilet paper*: To avoid rashes and itchy skin take along tissues or toilet paper. Use the garbage bag for used tissues.

5. *Sunscreen*: Look for a brand that has a UVA/UVB protection of 15 or more. Read the label carefully and reapply after swimming if needed. (See Safety Alert on page 29.)

6. *A hat*: Hats protect the head and face from sunburn and the eyes from harmful rays. Even on a hazy day, the sun can cause sunstroke.

7. *A raincoat*: Take a lightweight nylon raincoat in case of an unexpected shower or if it's windy or cooler than forecast.

8. and 9. *A notebook and pencil:* Keep track of the day's events, record unusual sitings, draw sketches, and jot down landmarks, such as road names, so you won't get lost.

10. *A yogurt tub with holes in lid*: Collect insects along with grass or leaves so they will have a comfortable home until returned to the wild.

11. *Insect repellent*: A liquid or pump container is not harmful to the atmosphere and won't explode when heated. (See pages 138 and 139.)

12. *A penknife*: With an adult's approval, bring a knife for cutting roasting sticks and other uses. (See Knife Safety on page 117.)

13. *Matches*: With the waterproof matches on page 151, you'll always be able to make a fire. Check with an adult before using matches and see page 117 for how to put out a fire.

# DAY HIKE

**B**efore you head out for a hike, make a plan so you don't get lost, wander into a dangerous situation, or get covered in poison ivy. Here's a formula for a safe and stimulating hike.

## PLAN AHEAD

The National Park Service or the local chamber of commerce may sell very detailed local maps. You'll need one if you plan on a serious hike. A map indicates directions and points out cliffs, lakes, woods, and marked trails on public property.

You can walk an average of one mile per hour. Plan stops for eating, exploring, and lazing around. When you've decided the route, tell an adult where you're going and approximately how long the hike will take.

Hike with a friend and share the sights and sounds along the trail. If the hike is in the woods, leave five feet between you and your friend to avoid a branch in the eye. Try to walk quietly; you'll see more wildlife.

## WHAT TO TAKE

Turn to page 135 and pack the hiking essentials in the backpack. Also bring a snack and a watch. These few items will ensure a successful hike.

## WHAT TO WEAR

Listen to the radio weather forecast in the morning. Try to wear several light layers. It's better to take off extra clothes than to have too few. When dressing, keep in mind sun, bugs, poison ivy, and branches. A sun hat, cotton long-sleeved T-shirt, jeans, cotton socks, and comfortable running shoes are good hiking gear.

## RULES OF THE TRAIL

1. Garbage on the trail can harm wildlife as well as spoil the natural beauty. Leave the trail a cleaner place. Pick up the trash of other hikers.
2. Respect private property. Always get permission before walking on private land or beaches.
3. Take photos or sketch plants and animal life instead of removing them.
4. Stick to the trails. Blazing your own path will damage plant life and you might get lost.
5. Be home before dark.

# WATCH COMPASS

A watch can do more than tell when to be home for dinner. If you become lost, use it to make a compass. Once you know where north is, consult the map and you should be able to find the way home again.

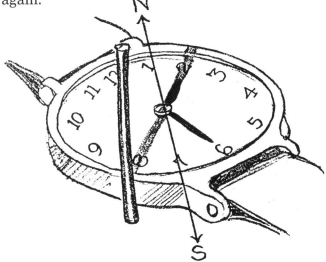

**1.**
Remove the watch from your wrist. Place it face up on a stone, making it as level as possible.

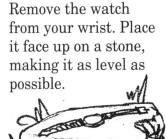

**2.**
Place a small twig on the edge of the watch face, opposite the hour hand. Rotate the watch until the stick's shadow lines up with the hour hand.

**3.**
North is exactly half-way between the hour hand and the number twelve. Always use the shortest way around the clock. For example, if it is two o'clock, north will point toward one, not seven.

**4.**
This compass works only on sunny days. If it's cloudy, look for moss, which always grows on the north side of tree trunks. Also, remember that the sun sets in the west.

# THE ITCHY PAGE

**W**ith the heat of summer come the bugs and plants that cause people to itch and scratch. Learning to identify the troublemakers could help avoid some uncomfortable situations.

## POISON IVY

Poison ivy has three pointed, shiny, dark green leaves with jagged edges and slightly hairy undersides along with gray-white berries. Poison ivy usually grows in the shade but will grow in the sun, too. It can be a single, delicate plant or a woody vine that takes over a large area. Often the leaves are shiny, but they can be dull. However it appears, don't touch it.

The poisonous part of the plant is the oily sap. It can be spread by the smoke of burning plants, via the fur of pets, from clothing, or by touching the plant itself. If you think you've come in contact with poison ivy, wash the skin and clothes with soap and water right away.

You have a reaction to poison ivy if a rash of tiny, intensely itchy, watery bumps develops. Ask a pharmacist for the best drugstore cure. Native Americans rubbed the crushed stems of jewelweed on the rash. Jewelweed often grows alongside poison ivy and has yellow blooms that dangle down like earrings.

## NETTLES

Even the name sounds prickly. Nettles, boiled and eaten by early settlers, are harmless when they first sprout. However, the mature plants have hairy spikes on the leaves and stems that can give a nasty, stinging rash that feels like a burn. A pioneer cure for stinging nettles was to wash the rash with the sap from the dock plant. Watch out for nettles while exploring in marshy areas or along roadsides.

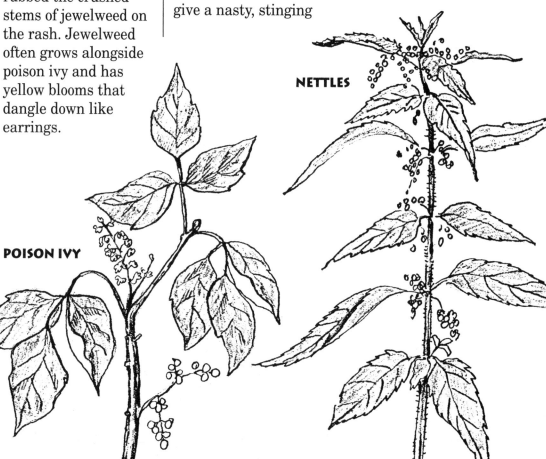

NETTLES

POISON IVY

## MOSQUITOES

It's nearly impossible to escape mosquitoes. They are attracted to warmth, moisture, dark clothing, and worst of all, carbon dioxide. So, as long as you're breathing, a mosquito can find you. Reduce the swarm buzzing for a bite by wearing light-colored clothing that covers as much skin as possible. A repellent can ward off bugs, too. Try citronella—it's an all-natural oil made from citrus fruits. You can buy it in most drug stores.

Instead of scratching, try to relieve the itch by dabbing it with lemon juice or rubbing it with a peeled garlic clove. A paste made with baking soda and water helps take the itch out, too.

## THE AMAZING MIDGE

Call them sand flies or midges. By any name, they give painful stings that cause very itchy, swollen welts. They are bloodsuckers, as are mosquitoes, but midges are so tiny they can pass right through clothing or a screen window to find a meal. Thankfully, midges often feed on mosquitoes. Nice to know mosquitoes can be bitten, too!

Midges breed near water or in rotting vegetation. If swarmed by midges, the only thing to do is run—for the citronella.

## BLACK FLIES

Memorial Day weekend coincides with the hatching of black flies, or buffalo gnats. Black flies are less than an eighth-inch long, but their vicious bite can leave a bleeding, itchy crater on the skin. Only the female black fly (and female mosquito) bite, in order to lay eggs. They live for three weeks so they get right to work looking for a blood donor. They will attack livestock, wildlife, people, and other insects.

Protect yourself from these blood hunters by wearing long-sleeved, long-legged clothing. They will attempt to climb under the clothing, so use an insect repellent around your wrists and ankles. Black flies are attracted to tender areas, such as the back of the neck, so put repellent there, too, and wear a hooded jacket.

# WILD SNACKS

**F**or a hike that's really on the wild side, take along a few wild snacks. Follow these safety rules, and the snacks will be nutritious, tasty, and safe to eat.

1. Use a field guide to identify plants and berries.
2. Never pick from the roadside, where the plants may have been sprayed with chemicals.
3. Never pick an area clean—leave plants and berries to reproduce.

# WILD BERRY LEATHER ROLLS

| You'll need: |
| --- |
| 2 cups wild strawberries or blackberries |
| a bowl |
| a potato masher |
| a tray |
| a sprinkling of sugar |
| waxed paper |
| a jar |

**1.**
Mash the berries into a pulp with the potato masher.

**2.**
Spread the mashed berries on a tray and let them dry for several days.

(Ojibwa people used to lay the pulp on sheets of birchbark. To do the same, rinse bark that has already fallen off a tree.)

**3.**
When the pulp is dry, dust the "leather" with sugar.

**4.**
Roll it up like a jelly roll and cut it into easy-to-eat pieces.

**5.**
Carry the rolls in the backpack, wrapped in waxed paper. Store extras in a clean, dry jar on a shelf.

# WILD RASPBERRYADE

**You'll need:**

| |
|---|
| 4 cups wild raspberries |
| a large clean jar with a lid |
| 1 cup vinegar (pioneers used cider vinegar) |
| 2 clean pieces of cheesecloth |
| 2 saucepans of the same weight |
| 2 cups sugar |

**1.**
Pack half the berries in the jar and pour in enough vinegar to cover them. Put on the lid and leave the jar in a cool place for two days.

**2.**
After two days, pour the berries into a piece of cheesecloth.

Squeeze the piece of cheesecloth full of berries so that the juice oozes through the cloth into the jar. Discard the cloth and the strained berry pulp inside.

**3.**
Fill the jar again with the remaining fresh berries. Cover it and leave in a cool place for another two days.

**4.**
Squeeze and strain the pulp through another piece of cheesecloth and pour the juice into a saucepan.

**5.**
Pour 2 cups of sugar into a second saucepan and hold it in one hand. Pick up the first saucepan with the other hand and compare the weights. Add or remove sugar until the two pots are about the same weight.

**6.**
Add the sugar to the juice and boil for ten minutes. Stir occasionally.

**7.**
Cover and chill the juice in the fridge. To make raspberryade, add 2 to 3 tbsp of the mix to a glass of cold water or seltzer. It makes a wild thirst-quencher to bring hiking.

## BERRY BEWARE

Berries ripen in stages throughout the summer. In the North strawberries are ready in late June, raspberries by mid-July, and blueberries in August. Blackberries also ripen in mid-July, but if you keep picking them, the bushes will produce well into August.

Unfortunately, there are poisonous berries, too. Never eat unripe or unfamiliar berries. Make certain to use a field guide or ask a knowledgeable adult to direct the berry-feasting.

# BIRCHBARK BERRY BASKET

Use a field guide to identify birchbark on the ground or on a dead tree. If there is no birchbark nearby, see the directions for making it on the next page.

| You'll need: |
| --- |
| a 10-by-12-inch piece of birchbark |
| scissors |
| a ruler |
| a pencil |
| 2 whittled sticks the size of toothpicks (or 2 toothpicks) |

**1.**
If the birchbark is too stiff to bend, soak it for an hour in cool water.

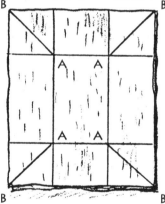

**2.**
Trim the piece of birchbark to the correct size.

**3.**
Using the ruler and pencil, draw four lines, each three inches from the outside edges of the bark.

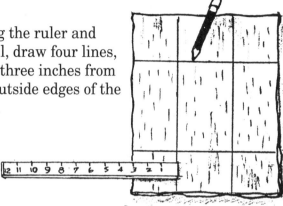

**4.**
The points where the lines intersect are points A and the corners are points B. Draw four lines from A to B as shown.

**5.**
Fold the bark and crease it along all the lines. To make the folds straight, line up the edges of the bark before making the crease.

**6.**
To form the basket, fold the corners as shown, overlapping the B points at the ends.

**7.**
Using the scissors, pierce two holes in each end of the basket, through all the layers.

**8.**
Insert the sticks or toothpicks into one hole and out the other. Now find a berry patch.

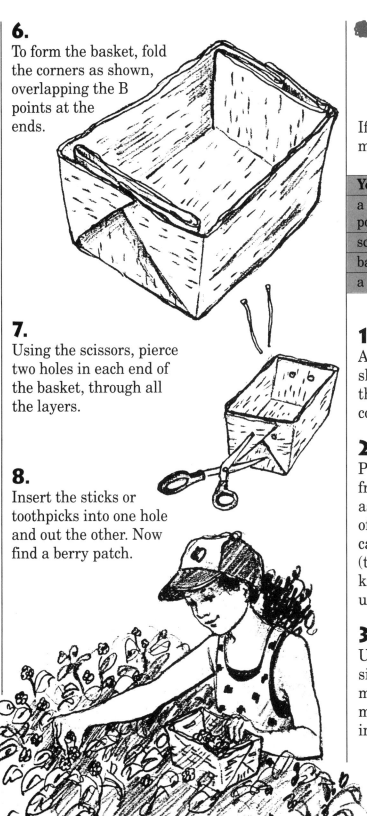

# MOCK BARK

If it is difficult to find birchbark on the ground, make a berry basket using cardboard.

| You'll need: |
| --- |
| a piece of thin cardboard (with one white side if possible) |
| scissors |
| bark or corrugated cardboard |
| a black crayon |

**1.**
A piece of cardboard from the packaging of new shirts or from a file folder is about the same thickness as birchbark. Cut the cardboard to the correct size, ten by twelve inches.

**2.**
Place a piece of bark found from another tree, such as oak, or a piece of corrugated cardboard (the ripply kind used to make boxes) under the cardboard.

**3.**
Using the black crayon, rub lightly on the white side of the cardboard. The lines created will make the cardboard look like birchbark. Use the mock bark to make a berry basket, following the instructions for the Birchbark Berry Basket.

143

# COOKOUT

**S**moke in the eyes, good smells in the nose, and fire crackling in the ears: it's a cookout. Everything tastes wonderful when you're the chef. All you need is a roasting stick, an open fire, and some food. (See page 114 for choosing a safe fire site and building a small fire.) Here are some scrumptious ideas for cookouts this summer.

## SMORES

| You'll need: |
| --- |
| marshmallows |
| a bar of chocolate |
| graham crackers |

Squishy and sweet, smores are an easy cookout dessert.

**1.**
Roast a marshmallow until golden brown.

**2.**
Make a gooey sandwich of marshmallow and chocolate between two graham crackers.

**3.**
Lick your fingers and say, "I want smore, please!"

# BREAKFAST BAKE

| You'll need: |
| --- |
| a knife and fork |
| an orange |
| an egg |
| an adult helper |

**1.**
Cut the orange in half and eat it.

**2.**
Pull out all the membranes to form an orange-rind poaching cup.

**3.**
Crack the egg into the cup.

**4.**
Use two sticks to gently lower the cup into the coals of a low fire. Cook for approximately five minutes. Eat the egg right from the rind.

# HOLE POTATO

Potatoes can be baked whole in a hole.

**You'll need:**

a potato and a stick

a penknife

butter (optional)

salt and pepper (optional)

**1.**
Before lighting the fire, scoop out a small pit in the ground.

**2.**
Wash the potato and poke it several times with the penknife. Toss the potato in the small pit.

**3.**
Cover the potato with ashes from a previous fire.

**4.**
Build the fire on top of the buried potato. The hole potato will take about an hour to cook.

**5.**
Let the fire die down before retrieving the potato with the help of a stick.

**6.**
Cut the potato open and add butter, salt, and pepper, if desired. Corn on the cob can be cooked using this method, too. Bake the corn in its husk.

# BANNOCK

Bannock, or wilderness bread, is flat and chewy and tastes great with butter and jam.

**You'll need:**

1 cup of flour

a big pinch of salt

2 tsp of baking powder

a bowl

a fork

1 tbsp of margarine

slightly less than 7 tbsp of milk

a frying pan

**1.**
Combine all the dry ingredients in the bowl.

**2.**
Use a fork to stir in the margarine and milk. Stir until most of the lumps are gone.

**3.**
With floured fingers, make a one-inch-thick loaf.

**4.**
Push the dough into an ungreased frying pan. Bake over a low fire for seven or eight minutes on each side, turning with a stick.

**5.**
Eat the bannock while warm, plain or with butter, jam, or peanut butter.

# SLEEP-OUT

If you've tried a day hike and a few cookouts and you're feeling outdoor-savvy, learn some wilderness skills, such as building a lean-to, starting a fire without matches, and weaving a comfortable bed—all from found materials.

The directions on the next few pages assume you have some of the essentials all good campers have—food, water, a good knife, a hatchet, and rope.

## NATURAL ROPE OR STRING

If you forget to take a piece of rope along, it's easy to make one. Find a dead cedar tree, cut off the outer bark, and then peel long strips of the inner bark still attached to the wood. Braid or twist the strips together to make rope. A piece of rope can be lengthened by tying some of the strips, over a bough, twisting them together, overlapping more strips, and adding them to the twist so the new strip is incorporated before the old strip runs out.

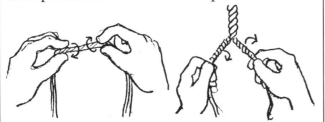

# CONSTRUCTING A LEAN-TO

Check out the area for materials to use for a lean-to. The site may have natural features that'll cut down on preparation and work. Trees that are the right distance apart, for instance, can be used instead of cutting and erecting poles.

**You'll need:**

a supply of poles, including a long ridge pole and 2 sturdy end poles—use only dead wood

rope

a supply of moss, boughs, and handfuls of dead, lichen-covered branches

knife or hatchet

**1.**
Build the lean-to in a sheltered spot so that the prevailing wind blows across the front opening. (See page 161 to find out how to tell wind direction.)

**2.**
Strip the poles of branches with a knife or hatchet. Remember to direct the knife strokes away from the body. (See Knife Safety on page 117.)

**3.**
A lean-to is begun with a skeleton of poles. Lash a ridge, or crossbar, pole between two trees or end poles and prop it up at each end with smaller poles, wedging it in place.

Lash the ridge pole high enough so that when more poles are laid on it at a steep angle, there is enough room underneath for a person to sit. A steeper angle makes a more waterproof lean-to. Leave the front of the lean-to open, but bank the two sides with poles.

## 4.

Once the skeleton is standing securely, stuff moss between the poles and then tie on dead boughs (stem up, underside facing out), one foot thick. Even better than boughs are handfuls of dead, lichen-covered branches held in place by a second row of leaning poles. Pack the two sides as well as the back of the lean-to.

# POSITIONING
## THE CAMPFIRE

Never build a campfire in front of the lean-to unless the opening is lengthwise to the wind, so that the wind blows onto one of the two sides of the lean-to. If the open mouth of the lean-to faces the wind, sparks and smoke will choke the living space. If the back of the lean-to faces the wind, air rising over it will create backdrafts with the heat of the fire, and smoke will be a problem again.

If the lean-to is situated correctly (so the prevailing wind blows across the opening), it's possible to build a small campfire in front of it, several long steps away. The smoke and sparks will drift past the opening, and a backdraft won't bring the fire or smoke dangerously close to the shelter. A campfire cooks food with the heat rising up with the smoke, but it warms you with the heat that radiates from the sides. Situated correctly, the fire will glow into the lean-to and give off a gentle warmth.

# BEDDING DOWN

**H**ere's how to make a comfortable mattress and bed frame for camping in the wild—or for reading a book close to home.

To make this bed, construct a simple but huge weaving loom that becomes the supporting bed frame.

| You'll need: |
| --- |
| a hammer |
| 2 strong nails at least 1½ inches long |
| a sledge hammer or good rock for pounding |
| 8 wooden sticks, about 1 inch thick and 1 yard long |
| a hatchet |
| 100 feet of strong cord cut into 16½-foot lengths |
| a good supply of bulrushes or reeds (or hay will do) |
| about 10 feet of sturdy string |
| an adult helper |

**1.**

Find two trees about one yard apart. Nail and lash one of the sticks between the trees to form a fixed crossbar, just less than one yard above the ground.

**2.**

Using the hatchet, sharpen one end of each of six remaining sticks so they can be easily driven into the ground. Ask an adult for help. Always chop or stroke with the hatchet blade directed away from the body.

**3.**

Pound the stakes partway into the ground, seven feet from the fixed crossbar and six inches apart.

**4.**

Lay the last stick on the ground behind the stakes, and ten feet from the fixed crossbar, parallel to it. This stick will become the free, moving crossbar of the loom.

## 5.

Tie one 16½-foot length of cord to an outside stake, loop it tightly around the fixed crossbar between the trees and pull it back to tie on the end of the free crossbar.

Repeat this procedure with each length of cord and each stake. Try to keep an equal distance between the cords on the fixed crossbar and an equal amount of tension between the crossbars. When you've finished, there will be six stationary cords running from the stakes pounded into the ground to the fixed crossbar. You'll also have six loose cords wrapped around the fixed crossbar and returning past the stakes and tied in six knots along the free crossbar. When the free crossbar is lifted, the loose cords attached to it lift, too, but the cords that run between the fixed crossbar and the stakes stay stationary.

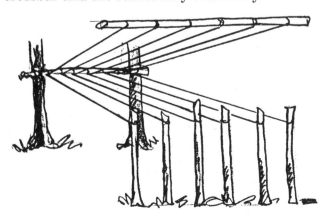

## 6.

Now it's time to weave. With an adult's help, raise the free crossbar up into the air to separate the loose and stationary cords, and place a bunch of rushes between them. Push the rushes evenly and tightly against the fixed crossbar.

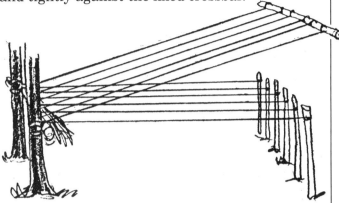

## 7.

Drop the free crossbar to the ground and lay another bunch of rushes between the cords. Squish them against those already woven in.

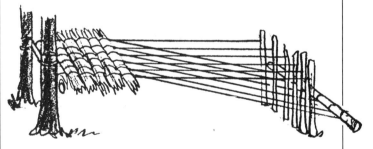

## 8.

Continue weaving in rushes by repeating steps 6 and 7 until the full length of the mattress is completed.

## 9.

Lash the free crossbar to the row of stakes with sturdy string to complete the bed frame and add extra support. Now lie back and enjoy the comfort of the handmade bed.

# MATCHLESS FIRE

Imagine that you're alone in the wilderness as night falls. It's cold and drizzling. You reach for the pack of matches to start a warm and friendly fire. Oh no!—they're soaking wet.

You can light a fire without matches or paper. All you need is a spark and lots of tinder. Practice at the next campfire. Then you'll know what to do in an emergency.

## FINDING THE BEST TINDER

Tinder can be the inner bark of dead trees, twigs shredded between the fingers, dead grass—anything that will flash into fire from just a spark. The best tinder is very dry, shredded into small pieces, and loosely packed.

If there is a meadow nearby, look for an abandoned bird's or mouse's nest in the long grass. The dried-out straw makes terrific tinder, as does

silk from milkweed pods, cattail fluff, and abandoned wasps' nests.

In an evergreen forest, look for brown, dried-up twigs on the lower branches of spruce, balsam, or cedar trees.

Even in heavy rain, there are dry dead twigs and bark low down on the tree trunks.

In a deciduous forest, look for coils of wispy birchbark on the ground. Birchbark is good tinder even when it's damp.

When there is enough tinder to form a small nest, make a campfire ring. (See pages 114–115.) Collect dry branches for kindling (see page 116) and pile them nearby so that once you have a flame, you can start feeding it.

## MAKING THE **SPARK**

Now it's time for a spark to set the tinder ablaze. Make a spark by striking flint and steel together. These rocks aren't hard to find. First, look for a glassy stone—quartz, agate, jasper, or flint will all work well. Choose a broken piece with a sharp edge. Then, find a piece of iron pyrite—also called fool's gold.

If iron pyrite isn't common in the area, anything made of steel will do. Use a pocket knife, nail file, or other small utensil made of steel.

Curl the tinder loosely into a nest in the center of the campfire ring. Strike the sharp edge of the flint stone with steel until sparks fall down into the tinder nest. If it's difficult to make a spark, try to keep the striking wrist as loose as possible.

When the tinder catches the spark, there will be a puff of smoke.

Then cup your hands around the nest and blow in quick, gentle puffs until there is a flame.

Slowly start adding small pieces of kindling to build a cozy, warm fire.

## WATERPROOF MATCHES

For an easy way to make a fire, always carry waterproof matches and a strip of sandpaper in a plastic bag.

Waterproof matches by bundling about ten wooden matches together and dipping them, including the tips, into melted wax. (See page 16 for how to melt wax.) Allow the wax to harden.

Keep them in a bag. When it's time to start a fire, separate one match, peel off the wax on its tip with your fingernail, and strike it on the sandpaper.

# RAINY DAYS

A summer day can be fun even if it's windy, cool, or raining. Relax inside and make a mask or a knotted bracelet. Try origami or construct a beading loom. Even learn how to forecast future nasty days. The activities on the following pages can turn the worst days outside into the best days inside.

# WEATHER WIZARD

**A**maze yourself and your friends by predicting tomorrow's weather today. Make the simple instruments in Sunny Highs (below) and Sunny Drys (see page 156), and use them to forecast sun or rain.

## SUNNY HIGHS

When air pressure is rising, good weather can be expected. When air pressure starts to fall, poor weather may be on the way. Find out whether air pressure is rising or falling by checking a barometer. Here's an easy way to make a barometer.

| You'll need: |
| --- |
| modeling clay |
| a flat-bottomed bowl |
| a ruler |
| a tall, narrow, clear plastic bottle |
| string |
| paper |
| pencil |
| tape |

**1.**
Stick a lump of clay on one side of the bottom of the bowl and use it to hold the ruler upright.

**2.**
Fill both the plastic bottle and the bowl three-quarters full with water.

**3.**
Cover the mouth of the bottle with one hand, turn it upside down with the other, and carefully lower the bottle into the bowl. When the bottle mouth is underwater, pull away your wet hand. Be sure to keep the bottle steady until it's balanced on the bottom and supported by the ruler. Don't put the bottle mouth into the clay.

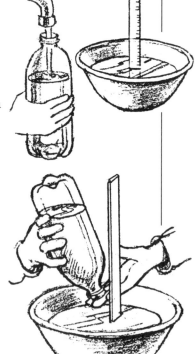

**4.**

Tie the bottle to the ruler with string in at least two places.

**5.**

Tape a strip of paper under the string, along the length of the bottle. With the pencil, mark a line on the paper to show the present water level inside the bottle.

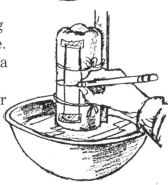

**6.**

Each day, check if the water level has changed from the day before. At the beginning of a clear, dry day, the water level inside the bottle moves up high. Mark the level of this "high" on the strip of paper. At the onset of stormy, wet weather, the water level inside the bottle will fall low. Mark the level of this "low" on the paper.

**7.**

Store the barometer in a cool place, away from the sun so that the water in it will not evaporate.

**8.**

To forecast the weather, check to see if the barometer is rising or falling. Note the water level periodically throughout the day. Expect good weather when the water level in the bottle is creeping toward "high"; rainy weather when the water level is dipping "low"; and unsettled, windy weather when the level is changing rapidly.

# HOW DOES IT WORK?

Even though we don't feel it, air in the atmosphere presses down on the earth all the time. Sometimes that pressure is a little stronger than at other times. In the barometer, the air presses down on the water in the bowl. When the air pressure is high, it pushes so hard that some of the water is pushed into the bottle, raising the water level in the bottle. When the air pressure is low, the opposite happens and the water in the bottle lowers. High pressure brings good weather, low pressure brings poor weather. A barometer forecasts what kind of weather is coming because air pressure starts to change before the weather does.

155

\* \* \* \* \* \* \* \* \* \* \* \* \* \* \* \* \* \* \* \* \* \*

# SUNNY DRYS

It's usually good weather when the air is dry. As moisture or humidity in the air builds, so does the chance of rain. Measure humidity by using this homemade hygrometer.

| You'll need: |
| --- |
| scissors |
| an 8-inch strip of colored, lightweight cardboard |
| tacks |
| a block of wood at least 8 by 1½ inches |
| a square of heavy cardboard at least 8 by 8 inches |
| tape |
| a straight human hair about 8 inches long |
| a felt-tip marker |
| a tiny ball of eraser or chewing gum |

**1.**

Cut an arrow from the strip of lightweight cardboard, as shown.

**2.**

Tack the wood block behind the stiff cardboard square to hold it upright.

**3.**

Tape one end of the hair to the top of the cardboard.

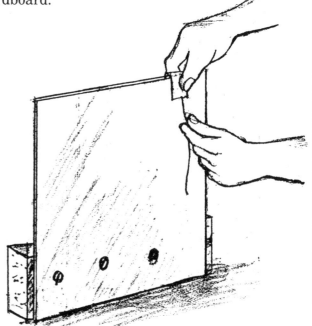

**4.**

Hold the arrow across the face of the board so the pointer lays over the loose end of the hair. Tack the blunt end of the arrow to the cardboard. (Stick a tiny ball of eraser or chewing gum over the sharp end of the tack so that it won't fall out.)

**5.**

Tape the loose end of hair to the back of the head of the arrow.

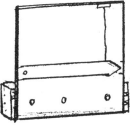

**6.**

On a dry, sunny day, mark where the arrow rests on the board with the word *dry*. On a rainy day, mark where the arrow rests with the word *humid*.

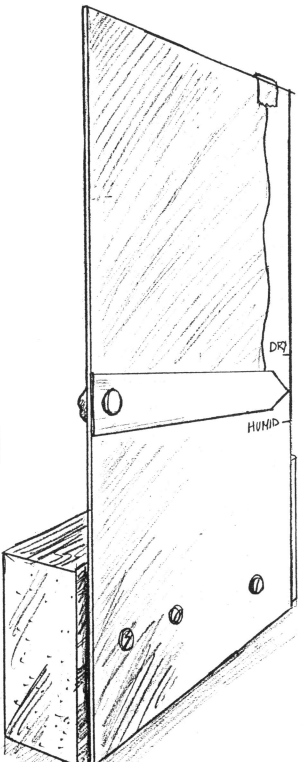

DRY

HUMID

## HOW DOES IT WORK?

Because human hair lengthens with moisture and shrinks with dryness, the arrow will drop a little if the air is humid and rise if it's dry. If the arrow drops to "humid" and the day is hot, watch for a thunderstorm. If the arrow rises to "dry," put away the raincoat for a while.

# NATURAL WEATHER REPORTS

**D**andelions can forecast the weather. On sunny days, the dandelion flower is open. But before it rains, the dandelion closes tightly so that none of its pollen gets wet.

Dandelions have a strong sensitivity to moisture. Pick a dandelion stalk, make a few slits in the bottom of the stem, and then put it in water. Before long, the ends of the stem curl up and the dandelion flower head pulls up tightly.

Like dandelions, most wildlife seem to know when good or bad weather is coming. Watch for some of the plant and animal behaviors on this page to forecast rain or shine.

## FAIR WEATHER COMING

- geese, crows, and swallows fly high

- fishing is poor

- ants scurry

- pinecones open

- dandelions open

- marigolds open

## FOUL WEATHER COMING

- birds fly low and line up on wires

- fish bite
- flies bite

- ants travel in lines

- pinecones close

- dandelions close

- milkweed pods close

## WILDLIFE AND THUNDERSTORMS

Become aware of how the natural world reacts to an approaching summer thunderstorm and you'll know when to take cover. If you first notice the storm when the sky begins to darken, think about it. You've probably been aware of little changes for at least an hour. You may have noticed that everything smells more strongly— even lake water smells before a storm. If you're near a campfire, the smoke may have been bothering the eyes—another sign of poor weather on the way.

The storm is still a few minutes away if birds are noisy, active, and restless, and if insects are busy biting. But when the birds suddenly disappear and all is strangely quiet, take immediate shelter or get soaked.

## CRICKETS CHIRP OUT THE HEAT

A cricket chirps depending on the heat: it chirps more when it's hotter. You can tell the temperature by counting the number of chirps heard. All that's needed is a watch and a chirping cricket. Here's what to do:

**1.**
Count the number of cricket chirps heard in fifteen seconds.

**2.**
Add forty to this number. The answer is the temperature in degrees Fahrenheit.

Suppose it's hot outside, and there are forty chirps in fifteen seconds.

$$40 + 40 = 80°F$$

Now that's heat with a beat!

# WEATHER PROOFS

**T**he methods on the last few pages will help you forecast the weather correctly most of the time, but there will be days you'll be fooled.

Set up a weather recording system to track the true weather. Keep records of temperature, rainfall, and wind on a calendar in order to compare statistics day to day.

## TEMPERATURE

Whether using a cricket thermometer (see page 159) or a thermometer on the wall, record the temperature at about 1:00 P.M. to determine the daily high. (The daily low is usually at 3:00 A.M., when most people are asleep.) Write down the daily high on the calendar to be able to tell which day was the hottest.

## RAINFALL

A narrow, sturdy tin can placed in an open area will collect daily rainfall. Right after a shower or storm, before any rain evaporates, take a ruler to the can, measure the number of inches that fell, and record that number on the calendar. If the amount collected is so small it can't be measured, use *T* for *trace* on the calendar.

# WIND

In 1858 an Englishman named Admiral Francis Beaufort invented a scale to measure wind force by noting the effect of wind on trees. Use the Beaufort scale to record the wind force.

**Force 0**
Calm. Leaves, branches, trees stand still.

**Force 1–3**
Light breeze. Leaves and small branches move.

**Force 4–5**
Moderate wind. Small trees sway.

**Force 6–7**
Strong wind. Big trees sway.

**Force 8–9**
Gale. Leaves and twigs snap off trees.

**Force 10–11**
Storm. Large branches break off trees, widespread damage.

**Force 12**
Hurricane or tornado. Large trees fall down, disaster.

Wind statistics usually include wind direction as well as force. Once you know where north, south, east, and west are, find a flag or a bending tree and then decide from which direction the wind is blowing. A flag or tree blowing toward the south is pushed there by a wind driving from the north, called a north wind.

If there isn't a flag or bending tree to look at, figure out wind direction by using the body. Lick the end of one finger and hold it up high. The side that feels coolest will face the direction the wind is blowing.

# WEATHER ROCK

If you prefer simplicity, there's always the weather rock. A weather rock is any rock placed out in the open. If the rock is wet, the weather is wet. If the rock is cold, the temperature is cold. If the rock is warm, the temperature is warm. If the rock is buried in snow, it's been snowing. If the rock is blowing away—watch out!

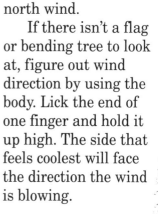

# FAN-TASTIC

**W**hat's the best way to beat the heat? Jump in the lake or take a breezy bike ride? Read the hot-weather tips on this page, then make this fan on a rainy day so you'll be ready to fan away the heat when the sun shines again.

Dress in lightweight, light-colored clothing, drink lots of water, and don't overexercise between 11:00 A.M. and 2:00 P.M., the hottest time of day. Animals feel the heat, too. Don't forget cats and dogs also need fresh water to drink.

Wildlife have their own ways of cooling down. When polar bears find the summer months too warm, they dig down into the permafrost, where it is always frozen, and curl up in an icy bed. Hippos spend the heat of the day submerged in a river, with nothing but their nostrils

sticking out. Many animals cool off with a swim, including bears, moose, wolves, birds, and even lions. Fish dive to deeper and colder water. Animals

also know to take a nap when it's really hot. From cats and dogs to chipmunks and sea gulls, the animal world lazes around from noon till four. One way you can beat the heat is to make a cooling fan.

**You'll need:**

| You'll need: |
| --- |
| a hammer |
| a small, sharp nail |
| 7 Popsicle sticks |
| a twist-tie |
| newspaper |
| scissors |
| heavy construction paper |
| felt-tip markers |
| white glue |

**1.**
Using the hammer and nail, make a small hole in the end of each stick.

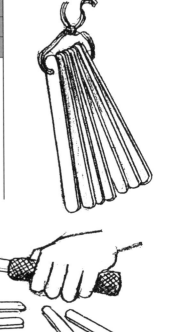

**2.**
Pull the twist tie through the holes of all the sticks. Make a neat loop with the twist tie and twist it to secure the sticks together.

**3.**
Spread the sticks out into a fan shape. Lay them flat on top of a piece of newspaper.

**4.**
Cut a curved strip of construction paper to form the top of the fan. It should be about four inches high, with the top measuring about eight inches and the bottom six inches.

**5.**
Decorate the paper with the markers.

**6.**
Glue the construction paper to the top of the fan. Allow it to dry. This is a fan-tastic way to keep cool.

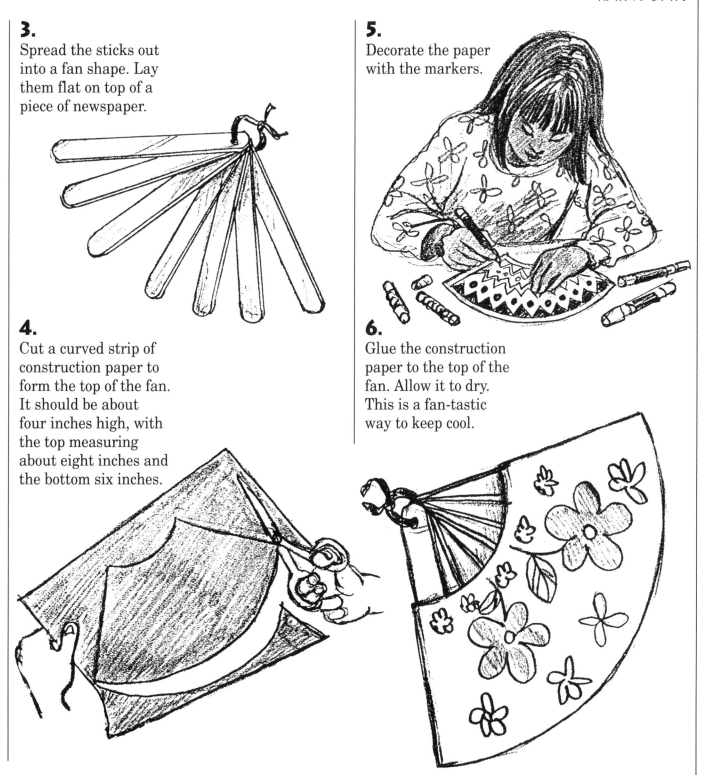

# RAINY-DAY GAMES

**B**righten up those dull, rainy days with a boxful of games.

## SHOWERY SHUFFLEBOARD

| You'll need: |
| --- |
| a ruler |
| a pencil |
| a 24-by-32-inch piece of cardboard |
| 4 pennies |

**1.**

Using the ruler, draw a triangle with one point in the middle of the cardboard. Divide the triangle into sections with points ranging from 5 to 15, as shown. Make two -1 sections for when players fail to get on target.

**2.**

Draw a line two inches from the opposite end of the board. Don't allow the hand to cross over this line when taking a shot.

**3.**

The two players decide to be heads or tails and take two pennies each. Heads goes first.

**4.**

Place the game board on a table or floor. Heads slides the penny back and forth and then releases it at the line, aiming for the triangle. Tails takes a turn, also aiming for the triangle. Keep taking turns until someone scores 100 points. (Hint: Try to knock the opponent's pennies out of the triangle. If any are knocked into the -1 section, that player loses a point.)

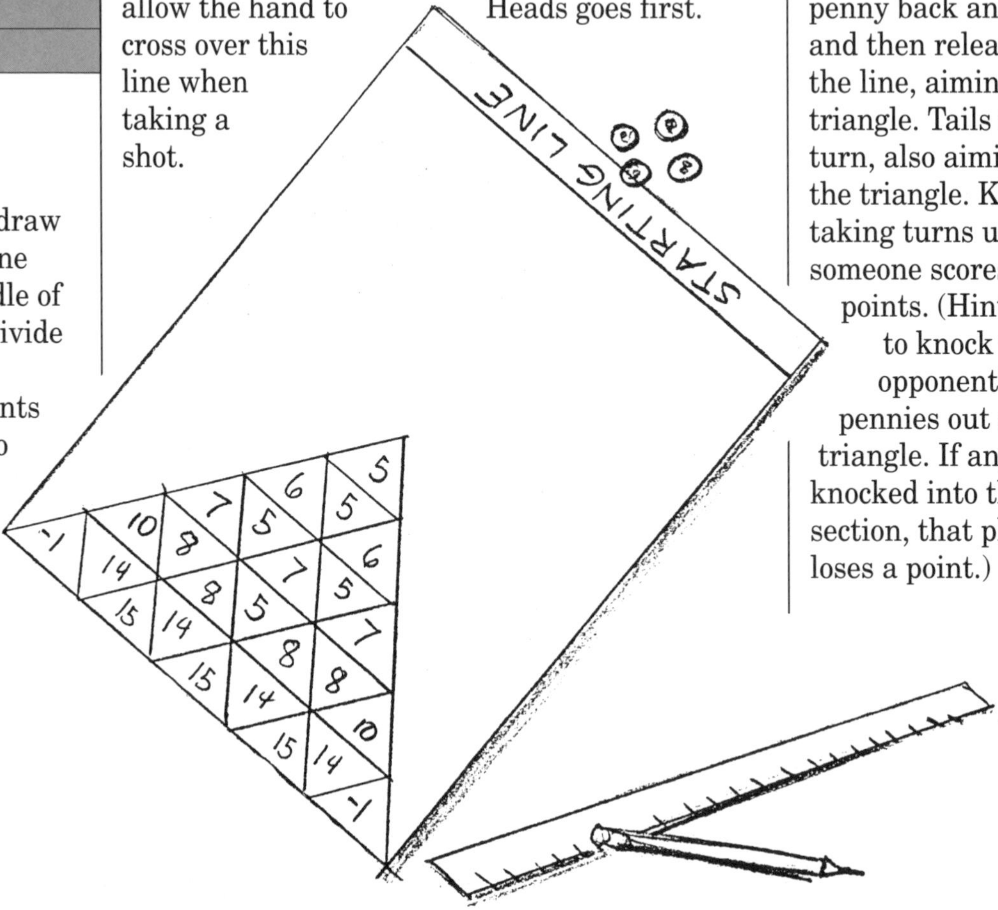

# THUNDERSTORM TRAY GAME

**You'll need:**

25 small objects

a tray

a dish towel

pencils

paper

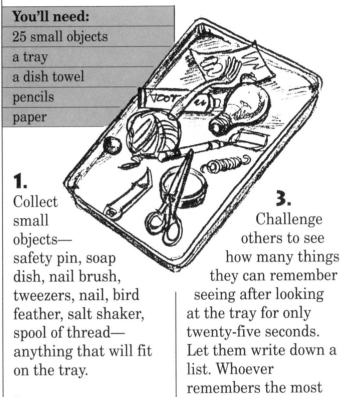

**1.**
Collect small objects—safety pin, soap dish, nail brush, tweezers, nail, bird feather, salt shaker, spool of thread—anything that will fit on the tray.

**2.**
Place the objects on the tray and cover it with a dish towel.

**3.**
Challenge others to see how many things they can remember seeing after looking at the tray for only twenty-five seconds. Let them write down a list. Whoever remembers the most items wins.

**4.**
Ask them to challenge you with a different assortment or have them remove some of the objects and you try to quickly guess what's missing.

# SOLITARY HOURS

**You'll need:**

a deck of cards

**1.**
Set up the game by making a clock shape. Starting at one o'clock, lay down one card at a time in a clockwise direction—one, two, and so on, until twelve. Place a card in the middle. Continue to lay down cards until all thirteen piles have four cards.

**2.**
Starting in the middle, pick the top card. If this is a 3, place it next to three o'clock and take the next card from the top of the three o'clock pile. Jacks are 11, queens are 12, and kings are 13.

**3.**
Continue until all four kings appear in the middle. Then it is time to redeal. See how many cards can be picked before the last king turns up.

# PAPER-FOLDING

**L**earn the traditional Japanese art of paper-folding, or origami, and turn a scrap of paper into a leaping frog, an elegant swan, or a delicate boat.

For more origami ideas, borrow a book on the art of paper-folding from the library and try more complicated figures. The instructions on these pages will cover some of the basics needed to continue creating origami art.

| You'll need: |
| --- |
| scissors |
| paper—uncrumpled and crisp is best, but newspaper will do |
| a ruler |

## 1.

For folding a frog, cut paper 2½-by-4 inches. For making a swan, cut paper six inches square. For a boat, use a piece of letter paper—8½-by-11 inches. Trim the edges so the measurements are exact on all sides and the angles are square.

frog
2½" x 4"

swan
6" x 6"

boat
8½" x 11"

## 2.

Follow the diagrams, using this symbol key:

↓ **valley fold** (the valley fold points away from you)

↑ **mountain fold** (the mountain fold forms a ridge pointing toward you)

**crease** (a crease is a line on the paper made by making a fold and then opening it up flat again)

**turn over** (turn the paper over before making the next fold)

**3.**
Fold, crease and turn the paper as the diagrams direct, working in the order indicated by the numbers. Remember to set up each fold carefully, with corners matching and edges meeting. Rub a fingernail along every fold, so the line is clean and sharp.

**FROG**

**SWAN**

**BOAT**

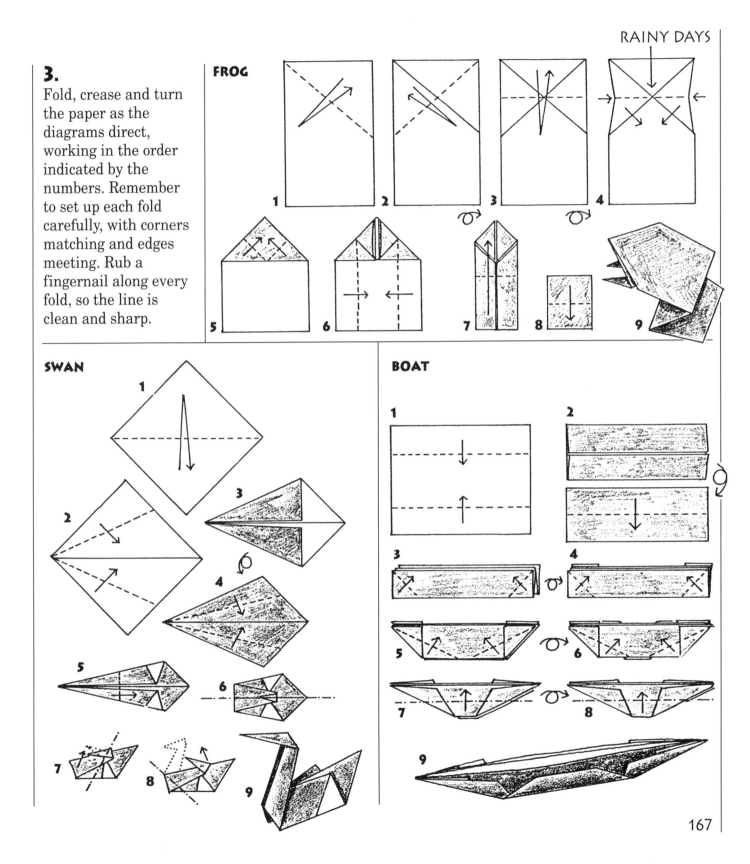

167

# BEADING LOOM

**B**eading is a handicraft that is fun to do, especially with your own loom. Make bracelets, anklets, headbands, and bookmarks, or decorate belts and backpacks.

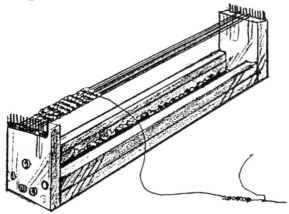

| You'll need: |
| --- |
| a handsaw |
| a 5-inch-long fine-toothed comb |
| a hammer and nail |
| sandpaper |
| 2 pieces of wood, 4 inches by 3 inches |
| a screwdriver |
| 14 wood screws |
| wood glue |
| 2 pieces of wood 14 inches by $3/4$ inch |
| a 14-by-3 inch piece of wood |
| white polyester thread, or elastic thread for bracelets and rings |
| tiny beads |
| a beading needle (very thin) |

**1.**
With the help of an adult, carefully saw the comb in half. Use the hammer and nail to make holes in the plastic handles of the two combs a half-inch from each edge.

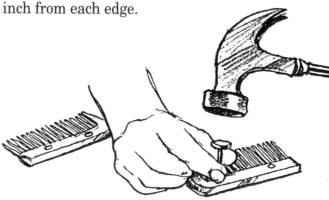

**2.**
Sand all the pieces of wood until they are smooth.

**3.**
Attach the combs to the small pieces of wood by placing the handle of each comb a half-inch below the top, so that the teeth of the comb protrude above the edge. Screw the comb into the wood through the holes in the plastic handle.

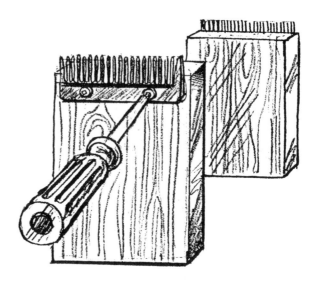

**4.**

Glue the two 14-by-³/₄-inch pieces of wood to the edges of the larger piece. Allow them to dry. This creates a well in the middle of the loom to catch fallen beads.

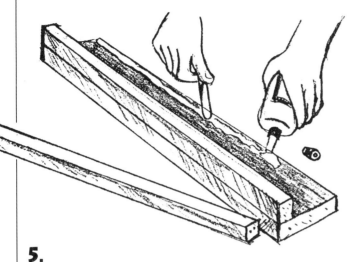

**5.**

Attach the small pieces of wood with the combs to the glued pieces, using four screws on each end as shown.

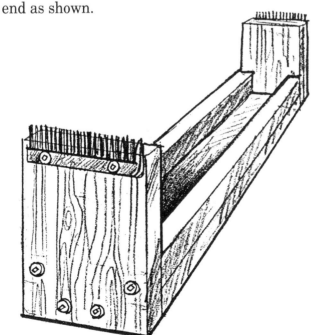

**6.**

To secure the threads, position one screw in the middle of each end, three-fourths inch above the bottom. Screw halfway into the wood.

**7.**

To thread the loom for creating a bookmark an inch wide, cut eleven pieces of thread, twenty inches long.

**8.**

Wind each thread around one middle screw, through the teeth of one comb, directly across the loom, through the other comb, and around the other middle screw. Proceed with the adjacent set of teeth until an inch of the comb is threaded. Turn the page to find out how to start beading.

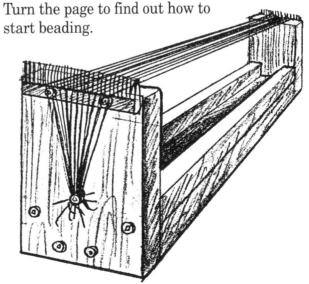

# B E A D I N G

Once the loom is ready (see page 168), begin the first beading project. Choose beads and place them in a small, heavy bowl.

## 1.

Thread the beading needle with about a yard of thread. If the eye of the needle is too small for the thread, stretch it wider using a pin or needle. Do not double or knot the thread.

## 2.

Place the loom between the legs, with one comb at the knees and the other near the stomach.

## 3.

Knot the beading thread to the outside left-hand thread of the loom.

## 4.

Pull ten beads through the needle and onto the beading thread.

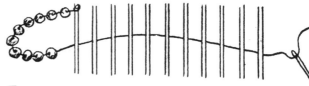

## 5.

Place the needle underneath the loom threads. Use a finger to position each bead between two loom threads.

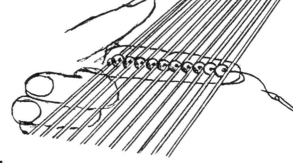

## 6.

Draw the needle through the bead holes from right to left, above the loom threads.

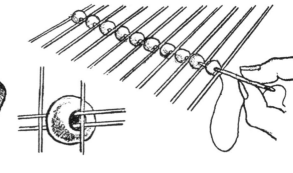

## 7.

Keep the beading thread taut. The row of beads should lie flat between the loom threads.

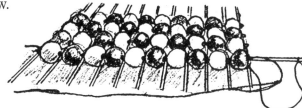

**8.**

Continue to weave beads exactly as for the first row.

**9.**

To change needle thread, weave the end of the first thread into the previous rows and remove the needle. Cut a new piece of thread, rethread the needle, and run the needle through several rows of beads. Knot the second thread around the outside loom thread and continue from where you left off. Keep beading until the bookmark is the length of a paperback book.

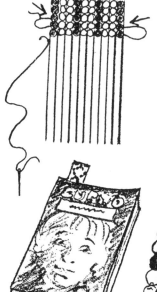

## FINISHING OFF

When the project is finished, secure the threads to prevent the beads from unraveling.

**1.**

To make a fringe, remove the threads from the screw at one end. Start at one edge and thread the first loom thread with the beading needle. Pull the needle through eight beads, then, bypassing the eighth bead, loop back through the other seven beads. Weave in the excess thread and trim. Repeat for all the loom threads.

**2.**

To make a straight edge, simply weave the remaining needle thread through the work. Untie the loom threads from the screw and work each one into the beading and trim. Now sew the design onto a backpack, hat, or belt.

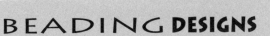

## BEADING **DESIGNS**

Once you have the hang of beading on a loom, create your own designs. Use graph paper and colored pencils to sketch out designs. A personalized bookmark is easy to make. Highlight your name in one color and make the background another color.

171

# KNOTTING BRACELETS

**S**pend a lazy afternoon making an easy, fun-to-wear bracelet with a safety pin and colorful embroidery thread.

| You'll need: |
| --- |
| scissors |
| 3 colors of embroidery thread |
| a safety pin |

**1.**
Cut six strands of embroidery thread, two of each color and about an arm's length each.

**2.**
Put the ends of the threads together and tie them in a knot to the safety pin.

**3.**
Attach the safety pin to the knee of your jeans or a pillow. Pull the strands of thread toward the body and adjust the knot so the threads lie flat on the lap.

**4.**
Think of the left thread as 1, the thread to its immediate right 2, then 3, and so on to 6.

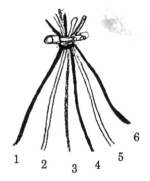

**5.**
Hold 1 in your right hand.

**6.**
Put your left hand under 2 and pull it down with four fingers. At the same time, stick up your left thumb so it juts between threads 1 and 2.

**7.**
With your right hand, pick up 1, pull it in front of your left thumb and across 2. There should be a right-angled triangle or L shape made from thread 1 crossing 2.

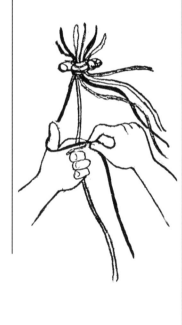

**8.**
With 1 still crossing over the top of 2, slip it around and under 2, and then up through the center of the triangle. Pull 1, releasing the left thumb while tightening the knot toward the safety pin.

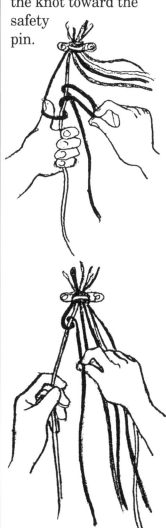

**9.**
Make a second knot on top of the first with threads 1 and 2. These two knots make a stitch.

**10.**
Now, lay thread 2 over to the left, pull 1 straight down and hold thread 3 with the four fingers of the left hand. Stick up your left thumb so it juts between 1 and 3. There is a front and a back to the bracelet, so don't let the stitching flip over—always work on the same side.

**11.**
Repeat steps 5 to 7 for threads 1 and 3, and then start to work with 1 and 4.

**12.**
Continue until thread 1 has been stitched with all the others and then straighten out the results. Thread 2 should now be the first thread on the left. Treat it as 1 and repeat steps 4 to 9.

**13.**
Continue to work the pattern until the bracelet just fits around the wrist. Get a friend to tie it on and leave it on all summer. A knotted bracelet will keep looking great—swim after swim.

**14.**
After some practice, try creating different effects by using some threads of the same color or by increasing to nine strands across.

173

# MASK-MAKING

**A** mask can be made from a paper plate, a paper bag, or an old pair of sunglasses, but a mask that is molded to the true shape of your own face is much more interesting. Here's an easy way to make a face-fitting mask to give yourself a fantastical look.

| You'll need: |
| --- |
| scissors |
| kraft paper or paper torn from heavy brown grocery bags |
| a mirror |
| a toothpick |
| white glue |
| newspaper |
| watercolor paints |
| a paintbrush |
| seeds, feathers, pebbles, dried mushrooms, string, bottle caps, stamps, pine needles, pasta pieces, and other found materials for decoration |

**1.**
Cut a strip of kraft paper about a half inch wide and long enough to make a headband across your forehead and around the back of your head. Look into the mirror, and using the toothpick as a gluestick, glue it to fit. Be careful not to get glue on your face or hair.

**2.**
Cut three more strips of half-inch wide paper. Look in the mirror, fit, and glue one strip to circle from the headband in front of one ear, around the front of your chin and up to the headband in front of your other ear. Arrange the other two strips to form a cross on top of your head, one running front to back of the headband and the other over the top from ear to ear. Let the glue dry.

**3.**
Cut about ten quarter-inch strips of paper. Looking in the mirror, glue one piece to run from the chin strap below one ear, up and over the bridge of your nose to the chin strap, just below your other ear. Guide the paper so that it follows the dips and hollows of your face as accurately as possible. A friend may be helpful with this.

**4.**

With the other quarter-inch strips of paper, complete the framework of the face, running strips from the front of the headband down the nose to the bottom of the chin strap, and across the face attaching onto the chin strap. Continue to shape the strips to the face. Leave large openings for eyes, nostrils, and mouth.

**5.**

Work the mask off your face by the headband and set it on a crumpled ball of newspaper about the size of your head. Let it dry completely.

**6.**

Tear narrow strips of kraft paper, and with the mask back on your face, attach them to the framework. Glue the paper, always pressing gently with the fingers and thumbs so the paper finds the contours of your face. Keep adding strips of paper until the form of your face is made.

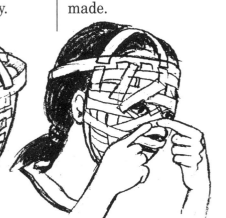

**7.**

Take off the mask and let it dry again on the newspaper ball. Trim around the eyes and adjust the other features as desired.

**8.**

With the mask back on your face and looking in the mirror, keep adding and interlacing layers of paper until the structure is strong and rigid. Let it dry completely on the newspaper ball.

**9.**

Paint and decorate the mask to look lifelike, funny, horrifying, or weird. Put it on and look in the mirror. Is it you?

# COTTAGE CRAFTS

There are lots of interesting natural materials for arts and crafts around the cottage. Prepare fabric dyes from wild plants and use them in printmaking or weaving. Or find some natural clay and form a pot. Why not whittle away an afternoon? Look in this section for lots of ideas for nature crafts.

# FRUIT DRYER

**Y**ou don't have to live in California to make raisins. This fruit dryer can dry fruit for snacking, or hikes, or anywhere.

| You'll need: |
| --- |
| a penknife |
| a rectangular cardboard box |
| a pencil and a ruler |
| cheesecloth or gauze |
| tape |
| aluminum foil and plastic wrap |
| a darning needle and string |
| apples and grapes |
| an adult helper |

**1.**
Carefully cut off the box top.

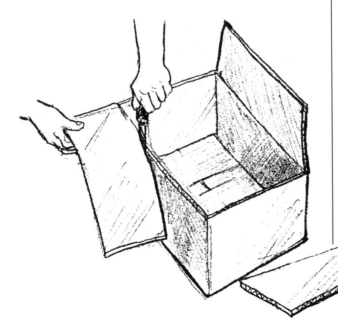

**2.**
With the pencil, label the sides of the box: back, front, left, right, and bottom.

**3.**
Using the ruler, draw a line from the back top corner of the box to the lower front corner on the left and right sides.

**4.**
Cut along the line.

**5.**
Cut along the bottom seam of the front side. Remove and discard the front section of the box.

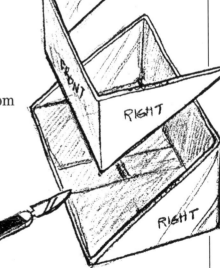

**6.**
Cut a triangular window in the left and right sides of the box.

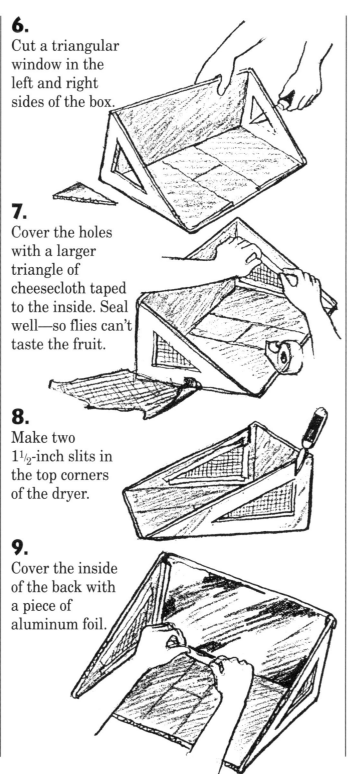

**7.**
Cover the holes with a larger triangle of cheesecloth taped to the inside. Seal well—so flies can't taste the fruit.

**8.**
Make two 1½-inch slits in the top corners of the dryer.

**9.**
Cover the inside of the back with a piece of aluminum foil.

**10.**
Thread the darning needle with string, and string thinly sliced apples and grapes.

**11.**
Hook the string into the slits in both upper corners, letting the fruit dangle into the dryer without touching the bottom.

**12.**
Cover the dryer with a piece of plastic wrap. Seal with tape if needed.

**13.**
Place the dryer in the sunshine. Bring it indoors at night. Drying will take two to three days.

# PLANT FABRIC DYES

**C**olors found in nature are often soft and warm—yellows, pinks, and browns. Native and pioneer people used nature's palette to color the cotton, wool, and linen fabrics they wore. Create these natural dyes using a variety of plant parts—berries, twigs, flowers, stems, and vegetable skins.

The first step is to find out which plants are available in the area. Look for bright flowers, berries, and leaves. The dyes won't be as bright as the colors of the plants. The dyed fabrics will be will be lighter in color and some plants are tricky—red onion skin makes a muddy-green dye!

## COLOR CHART

| Plant | Color of dye |
|---|---|
| sunflower | soft yellow |
| goldenrod | yellow/beige |
| wild rose hips | oatmeal brown |
| blue lupine | pale green |
| oak bark | dark brown |
| wild holly berries | pale pink |
| black walnut (shells) | very dark brown |
| onion (skin) | yellow |

| You'll need: |
|---|
| an apron to protect clothes |
| 8 cups of water |
| a large bowl of plant pieces broken into small bits |
| a large pot |
| a stove |
| cotton string, natural wool, or cotton T-shirt |
| a wooden spoon |
| an adult helper |

**1.**
Ask an adult to help combine the water and plant pieces in a large pot.

**2.**
Slowly bring to a boil and boil gently for one hour.

**3.**
With fresh water, wet the string, T-shirt, or any fabric to be dyed. Squeeze out excess water and then add to the pot.

**4.**
Boil for half an hour, stirring occasionally with a wooden spoon.

**5.**
Remove pot from the heat and allow to cool.

**6.**
Remove the dyed fabric from the pot, wring out, and hang outside to dry.

**7.**
Compost the boiled plants.

# GOD'S EYE

The naturally dyed string can be used in many crafts and string games. Try making a God's eye using several colors of dyed string.

**You'll need:**

2 sticks about the size of Popsicle sticks

white glue

dyed string

a pencil

hollow pasta (optional)

**1.**
Make a cross or small t with the sticks.

**2.**
Glue the sticks together.

**3.**
When the glue is dry, tie the end of the string where the sticks meet. The knot should form an X on the front. The side where the knot is tied becomes the back.

**4.**
With the pencil, mark the four arms of the sticks with the letters *A, B, C,* and *D.*

**5.**
Hold on to stick D, loop the string up and over stick A and bring the string up between sticks B and C. Loop the string up and over stick B and bring the string up between sticks C and D.

**6.**
Continue working counterclockwise. Hollow pasta, shells, or beads can be added at intervals.

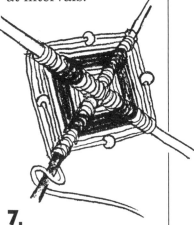

**7.**
To add a second color of string, tie it to the end of the first string.

**8.**
Hang the God's eye in a window with a piece of string and it will turn in the breeze, decorating the room.

# PLANT PRINTS

**S**how off the natural dyes (see page 180) by making prints with natural patterns.

| You'll need: |
| --- |
| newspapers |
| white fabric—an old sheet, pillowcase, or dish towel |
| natural dye (see page 180) |
| a pan |
| plants with interesting shapes, such as the Queen Anne's lace flower, beech leaves, maple bark |

**1.**
Spread newspapers over the work area.

**2.**
Lay the fabric flat over the newspaper.

**3.**
Pour some dye into the pan.

**4.**
Hold a freshly picked Queen Anne's lace flower by the stem and dip the flower into the pan.

**5.**
Let the excess dye drip into the pan.

**6.**
Move the wet flower over the fabric and set it down to make a print.

**7.**
Remove the flower and repeat the process to make a pattern. The fabric makes a great wall hanging.

# FISH PRINTS

Try this fishy print with the dyes. It's a traditional Japanese craft.

| You'll need: |
| --- |
| natural dyes (see page 180) |
| a paintbrush |
| a dead whole fish with scales |
| very thin paper or tissue paper (Japanese artists use rice paper) |
| a piece of smooth cardboard |
| glue—a gluestick is best here |

**1.**
Paint the fish head, body, scales, and fins with the dyes. Use many colors.

**2.**
While the dyes are still wet, put a sheet of tissue paper over the colored fish.

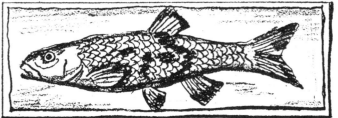

**3.**
Remove the paper and leave it to dry.

**4.**
Mount the finished work on a piece of cardboard. Dab the back of the print with a gluestick and stretch the fish print out smoothly over the cardboard.

## QUEEN ANNE'S LACE-MAKING

Queen Anne of England made beautiful white lace. People say that she always pricked her finger with the needle and left a drop of red blood on her work, and that's why the center of the white Queen Anne's lace flower is a tiny, bright spot of blood red.

# DRIED FLOWERS

If you've ever wished that summer would never end, keep it alive by collecting and drying flowers to make potpourri. Then, in January, take a breath of summertime.

There are two groups of plants that can be dried—flowers and grasses. For flowers, it's best to collect from a flower garden. Roses work best, but for a range of color collect delphinium, impatiens, and hollyhock. Very delicate wildflowers, such as violets, should be left in the wild. If the roots are disturbed, they won't grow again next year. Meadow flowers, such as pearly everlasting and Queen Anne's lace, are tougher plants. If they are very plentiful, pick a few, taking care not to damage the entire plant.

Grasses, from either the meadow or the swamp, should be collected in August when the plants are mature. Limit the number picked, taking only a few from each clump of plants. Use a field guide to avoid picking poisonous or endangered plants.

| You'll need: |
| --- |
| scissors |
| a variety of flowers and grasses |
| plastic bags |
| string |
| a cookie sheet |
| newspaper |
| a tray |

**1.**
Use a pair of sharp scissors to gather flowers and swamp grasses. Make a clean cut on the stem of the plant, taking at least six inches of stem. Snip roses off just below the flower.

**2.**
Collect four samples of each plant. Place each type in a plastic bag.

**3.**
On the picnic table or lawn, gather each type of plant into a small bunch and tie the stems with a piece of string, leaving about eight inches of loose string.

**4.**

Use the loose string to hang the bunches upside down to dry in a cool, dry place, such as a shed or garage. Tie them to a nail, pipe, or rafters. Avoid direct sunlight. If placed in the sun, the bright colors fade.

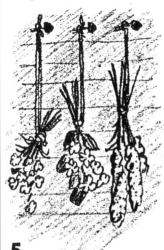

**5.**

Roses can be dried on a cookie sheet covered with newspaper. Remove the petals from the rose hip and spread them out on newspaper. Shake the cookie sheet every few days so the rose petals dry on all sides.

**6.**

The drying process will vary depending on the water content of the plant and the humidity of the air. They should all be dry in about two weeks. When the flowers are brittle, untie the string and remove the flowers from their stems. Collect all the dried flowers on a tray. Use your hands to mix them.

**7.**

The fragrance of the potpourri will depend on the varieties collected. Pearly everlasting and roses provide the strongest perfume. If the potpourri is too mild, add a few cinnamon sticks, cedar sprigs, or dried apples (see page 178) to liven up the scent. Potpourri can be kept in an open glass jar or a glass bowl.

## DRIED **ARRANGEMENT**

Dried teasels, grasses, and bulrushes can be arranged for permanent display. In a vase, old milk bottle, or large jar, arrange a few of each variety, placing the tallest at the back. Teasels can be painted or dusted in sparkles, or left natural.

# FLOWER-PRESSING

**W**atch for interesting plants in the area—some may have beautiful flowers and others may have unusual leaves. Here's how to make a plant press to preserve those shapes and colors for decorating postcards, notepaper, or invitations to friends.

| You'll need: |
| --- |
| 40 small flat sticks about the size of Popsicle sticks |
| white carpenter's glue |
| scissors |
| newspaper |
| an interesting assortment of plant parts |
| a small belt or length of rope |
| 2 six-inch-square pieces of plywood |
| a heavy rock |

**1.**

Lay out ten sticks in a row with tiny spaces between each one. Glue another ten crosswise over the row to make a lattice. Repeat to make a second lattice.

**2.**

Cut the newspaper into about eighty squares the size of the lattices.

**3.**

Pick twelve plant parts to press. (See page 187 for some ideas.) Use a field guide to avoid picking endangered or poisonous plants. Pick only a few of any one kind of plant.

**4.**

Now build the press. Lay the belt on the floor and place one plywood square on the middle of it. Lay down six squares of cut newspaper and place one plant on top. Arrange the plant as it should lay when it's pressed. Lay six more squares of newspaper on top, then the next plant, and repeat. Put a lattice after every four layers of plant and newspaper. After all twelve plants are stacked in the pile, place the second square of plywood on top and pull the belt tight around.

**5.**

Weigh down the press with a heavy rock and tuck it away in a dry spot for about two weeks (under the bed is a good place). Change the newspaper every couple of days to dry the plants faster, which keeps the colors bright.

## PRESSED-FLOWER POSTCARDS AND NOTEPAPER

Pressed flowers are very delicate, but gently gluing them onto blank cards and notepaper will help them last longer. To mail them, give them more protection. Cover them with sticky-one-side clear plastic from the hardware store.

### GOOD PLANTS TO PRESS

For best results, choose plants without thick or fleshy parts. Good choices include buttercups, daisies, wood ferns, forget-me-nots, violets, grasses, and colorful or interesting leaves.

# PLANT-WEAVING

**R**eed and rush leaves have been used to weave mats for hundreds of years. They can be made into sweet-smelling, natural placemats and coasters.

| You'll need: |
| --- |
| rubber boots |
| reeds and rush leaves |
| garden shears |
| a pail |
| newspaper |
| scissors |
| a ruler and a pencil |
| an X-acto knife |
| a sewing needle and thread |
| cardboard |
| an adult helper |

**1.**

Put on boots and take a walk to the edge of nearby water or swamp. Look for reeds, such as the common reed, and leaves, such as the leaves of bulrushes. Use a field guide to help find them. They must be green and easy to bend, not dried out, brown, or brittle. Use the shears to cut about twelve plants as close to the ground as possible. It's better to take fewer whole plants than to damage a lot of plants for smaller pieces. Carry the reeds home in a pail.

**2.**

Cover a table with newspaper and cardboard. Peel apart each plant layer by layer.

**3.**

Using the scissors, cut thirty reeds into twenty-inch lengths.

**4.**

Gently flatten each piece of reed with the edge of a ruler.

**5.**

To weave a placemat, all the reeds need to be about the same width. With an adult helper, use the ruler and X-acto knife to cut long rectangles of reed, about a half-inch wide.

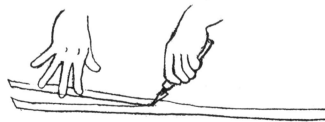

## 6.

Square off the top and bottom of each reed.

## 7.

Clear off the table and begin by laying fifteen reeds horizontally, leaving a space of a quarter-inch between each reed.

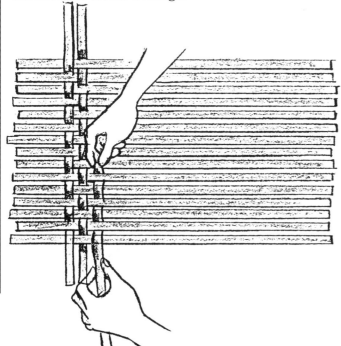

## 8.

Beginning at the left side of the mat, weave fifteen reeds vertically over and under the horizontal reeds. It's possible to add more reeds or to use fewer, depending on how big the mat is. Stop weaving about an inch before the ends of the reeds to make a fringe.

## 9.

With a pencil and a ruler, draw a faint straight line across the top and bottom of the mat. Use scissors to trim any reeds that are too long. Or leave it rough if desired.

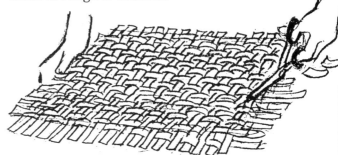

## 10.

To keep the mat from falling apart, you have to secure the four corners. Use needle and thread to sew an X in the corners or use a piece of vine or spruce root. (See page 146 for collecting natural string.)

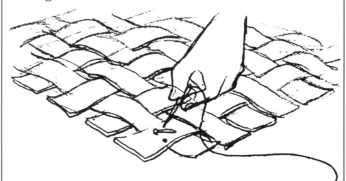

## 11.

Make as many mats as needed. Allow the mats to dry in the air. Don't store them in a drawer or cupboard until they are very dry.

## 12.

To make matching coasters, cut reeds into six-inch lengths and proceed as for the placemats.

# STRAW DOLLS

**C**reate a wild bunch of superheroes, villains, and animal monsters out of bits and pieces from the meadow and forest floor.

The original craft of making straw figures started centuries ago among the Iroquois in the eastern woodlands of North America.

Start by making bundled straw figures, and then add twigs, seeds, pods, and cones for special effects. Straw can be found in most fields and along roadsides. It is the pale yellow stalk left after uncut wild grass dies. When gathering straw, look for standing dead stalks with thick, sturdy tubes.

**You'll need:**

a dozen 12-inch tubes of straw

a pan or sink of warm water

a spool of thread

scissors

seeds, pinecones, bark, sticks, leaves

**1.**
Place the straw in warm water for an hour. It may have to be held down with a rock.

**2.**
Drain the straw for several minutes.

**3.**
Bundle twelve tubes of straw together in your hands. Just above the center of the bundle, circle with a length of thread and tie it to make a waist.

**4.**
Working with the longer section below the waist, separate the straws into two legs, and tie with thread at the top of the legs, the knees, and the ankles.

**5.**
Above the waist, at the neck area, bend two straws in half on each side to form arms. Tie at the neck, shoulders, elbows, and wrists.

**6.**
To make a head, bend in half four of the remaining straws above the shoulders and tie them down at the neck with thread. Tie again at the top of the head to make a headband.

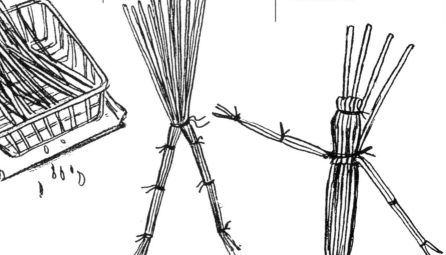

**7.**
Fan out four remaining lengths of straw, bend and tie at the neck as a cape and short, stand-up collar.

**8.**
Arrange the pose while the straw is still damp and then let the figure stand to dry.

**9.**
Decorate the character with flakes of bark, seeds, leaves, and other bits and pieces.

# STRAW ANIMALS

**1.**
Dampen and drain sixteen 12-inch straws, as described for the straw dolls.

**2.**
Bundle together eight of the wet stalks and tie at each end.

**3.**
About six inches from one end, bend up straw for a neck and tie thread around the joint. Move the hand up the neck and bend it down to form a head. Tie thread around this joint, too.

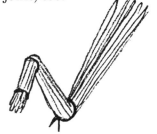

**4.**
With the remaining eight stalks, form two bundles and bend each in half over the body, and fasten with thread. Tie each leg at the knees and ankles, too.

**5.**
While the straw is still wet, arrange the neck and limbs so that the creature will stand up.

**6.**
Use bits of straw, seed husks, and other found pieces to make hair, manes, tails, ears, horns, antlers, and so on.

191

# CLAY WORKS

**C**lay is often found under the topsoil, along stream banks, or even underwater. A cool, smooth, easy-to-mold kind of mud is probably clay. Don't be confused by the color—clay can be brown, red, or gray. When you've collected a clump of clay, store it in plastic or under a damp cloth until ready to use.

## WORM POTS

| You'll need: |
| --- |
| a flat rock |
| a pail of water |
| clay |
| a small stick or toothpick |
| paints—watercolors, will do, but acrylics work better |
| a paintbrush |
| white glue or beaten egg yolk |
| a dull knife |

**1.**
Find a flat rock that can be comfortably used as a worktable and assemble the materials beside it.

**2.**
Wet the hands, tear off a lump of clay, and roll it between the palms, adding a little water if necessary, until the clay forms a ball.

**3.**
Flatten the ball with the palm of the hand, then trim with the knife until it looks like a large coin. This will form the base of the pot.

**4.**
Flatten another ball of clay on the rock with one wet palm and then roll the clay back and forth to form a long worm.

**5.**
Score the top and bottom of the worm with the toothpick or small stick. Scoring helps the sections of the pot stick together.

**6.**
Coil the worm around the base. Make sure one of the scored sides is touching the base. Smooth the coils with the thumbs and fill in any cracks and holes. Keep it wet.

**7.**
Make more long worms of clay, score them, and wind them around and up from the base until the pot is as tall as desired.

**8.**
Leave the worm pot out in the sun for a day or two until it dries hard.

**9.**
Once it's dry, paint the pot. Glaze it by brushing it with white glue or a little beaten egg yolk. The worm pot should not get wet, so only store dry things in it.

# JUMPING SPIDERS

| You'll need: |
|---|
| a flat rock |
| a pail of water |
| clay |
| 5 rubber bands, each snipped once to break the circle |
| a small stick |
| paints |
| a paintbrush |
| white glue or egg yolk |

**1.**
Roll two balls of moist clay, score, and push them together to form the main body parts of a spider.

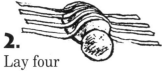

**2.**
Lay four cut rubber bands across the body.

**3.**
With wet thumbs and a little more clay, work the middle sections of the rubber bands into the spider body so the ends dangle beyond each side like eight legs.

**4.**
Turn the spider over and poke a hole through the center of the body with a small stick. Push the last piece of elastic into that hole and then work the clay to fill it back in.

**5.**
Find a sunny place to let the spider dry hard, carefully arranging the rubber bands so they can move freely.

**6.**
When the clay is completely dry, hold the rubber bands on the back and make the spider jump and wiggle its legs.

**7.**
Paint and glaze the spider. (See step 9 of Worm Pots.)

## WHAT IS CLAY?

Clay is actually rock ground to bits by wind, water, and ice. If pulverized rock collects in one place, such as at the mouth of a river, it may form sand, silt, mud, or clay.

Since the surface of the earth was once mostly water and rocks beating against each other, there's a great deal of clay lying on the bedrock and under the topsoil.

# FOSSIL IMPRESSIONS

**W**hile scrambling up a rocky hillside, walking in a gravel river bed, or kicking stones along a beach, it's possible to spot the tread of a tiny bulldozer pressed into the rock. Look again—it may be what's left of a trilobite. Three hundred million years ago, trilobites crawled along the bottom of shallow, warm seas, looking somewhat like crayfish or crabs. Today they exist only as fossils—the remains or impressions of prehistoric plants and animals that are embedded in stone. Here are some fossils to look for.

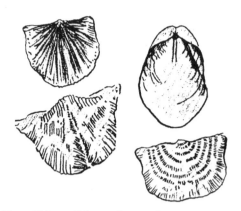

**Fossil brachiopods** are from a family of ancient shells. Some look like clams, some like stone butterflies, while others look like computer-game Pac-men with their mouths frozen open mid-munch.

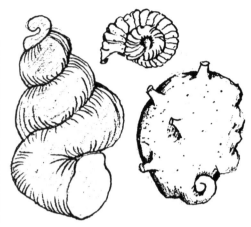

**Fossil gastropods** are prehistoric snails, with spiraling shell forms that are quite distinct. Some snail-shaped fossils are ammonites, the ancestors of the squid and octopus.

**Fossil corals** are found throughout the world because many places on earth were at one time shallow seas. A close look at fossil coral may reveal annual growth rings, just like those on the stump of a tree. Count the rings to guess how old the coral was when it died.

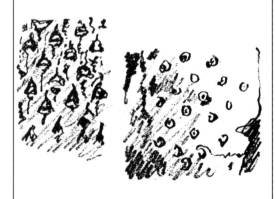

**Fossilized or petrified wood** is not exactly wood turned to stone. Instead, it's made of different compounds and minerals that filled and replaced the wood cavities as they rotted. Petrified wood can be yellow, red, orange, and other bright colors. Jewelers polish pieces of it to a gemlike shine.

# FOSSIL ART

Some fossils are sunken molds of prehistoric life—casts of shells or even footprints. Sometimes they're reliefs of plants or animals etched across the face of a rock. Other times the whole form protrudes. Here are some creative things to do with a fossil.

## RUBBINGS

A fossil on the surface of a rock, similar to the imprint on a coin, will make a great rubbing. Lay a piece of paper over the fossil and rub back and forth over it with a pencil, a piece of charcoal, or a crayon. Use repeated strong strokes for a detailed impression.

## EMBOSSING

Make an embossing of a protruding fossil with a coin and a sheet of sturdy aluminum foil. Look for foil used in a store-bought pie crust. Lay the foil over the fossil and rub back and forth with a coin. Display the finished product from either side.

## CLAY PRINTS

Fossils that protrude from the rock can be collected as a print on a clay tile. (See Clay Works on page 192.) Roll a slab of clay flat with a rolling pin or bottle. Shape the edges with a knife into the desired shape. Spread a little petroleum jelly over the fossil and press it into the center of the clay tile. Remove the fossil. Let the clay dry rock-hard before picking it up.

# ROCK ART

**G**ather some stones and take a good look at them. It may be possible to arrange them to make an animal or a sculpture. Or maybe one stone in the bunch can be made into something special. All over the world, people use ordinary rocks and stones in interesting and artistic ways. Here are some ideas to try with a rock collection.

## TRAIL SCULPTURES

On hiking trails, people often pile rocks to make landmarks and trail guides. These rock piles are called cairns. In some desert areas of the Southwest, people leave a short tower of flat, round rocks along the trail and then lay a pointed stone on top to indicate the direction to follow.

Cairns blend neatly into the surroundings. They are mysterious to follow—where will the wordless directions lead?

In the Arctic, Inuit people have turned trail-marking into an art. They construct rock markers to look like giant humans and call them *inukshuk*, which means "stone in the likeness of a person." Hundreds of years ago, the Inuit marked caribou migration routes with these *inukshuk* cairns.

Find rocks that can be piled so they stand together freely yet sturdily, clearly show a human form, and also indicate a direction. It's not easy—maybe that's why *inukshuks* make fascinating sculptures as well as trail markers.

# ROCK PAINTING

Look closely at a stone. Maybe, hidden in the stone, there is a shape that suggests a sleeping cat or a grasshopper tensed to jump.

In China, artists take lumps of jade and try to carve out the shape they see hidden inside, chipping off as little of the precious stone as possible. They aim to use all the contours of the stone to their best advantage.

Try to do the same with watercolor paint and a brush if the stone is smooth. Paint the stone to accentuate the details its shape suggests. Use a fine brush and lots of different colors, shades, and tints. When the paint dries, seal the work with beaten egg yolk or a thin coat of white glue. Or use a fine brush and different colors of acrylic paints, which leave their own gloss.

Now give this work of art a job to do. Maybe it can hold down napkins on the dinner table or letters from friends.

## ROCK GROUPS

Use white glue to hold stones together and create small scenes, animals, or even groups of people. What about a rock band? Or the people in your family? Mount these crazy creations on a piece of driftwood. Add bits of twig, evergreen needles, wool, and other special effects.

# WHITTLING

**E**very good wood-carver starts out as a whittler. With a sharp pocketknife and practice, it's easy to learn how to whittle. Just remember to hold the knife with the blade pointing away from the body. (Read about knife safety on page 117.)

## SOAP CARVING

| You'll need: |
| --- |
| a bar of pure soap and a knife |
| a flat wooden carving board |
| an adult helper |

**1.**
Place the soap on the carving board. Turn it several ways to get an idea of what to make. Some carvers, such as Chinese jade artists, look for a form in the material and believe their work is to cut away everything that is not part of that form. For example, you may see an owl shape in the soap.

**2.**
With a steady hand, and with the blade always moving away from the body, cut out the rough head and body shape of the owl. Cut off small slices at a time. Don't just work on the front view of the owl—cut to form an owl all around.

**3.**
Now work on details—face, wings, feet—but still cut small slices. Keep moving the soap around to continue to work on the whole owl shape.

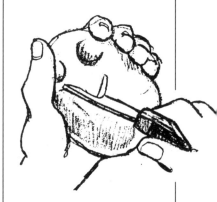

**4.**
Last of all, with the point of the knife, use lines to create finer details, such as feathers, eyeballs, and toes.

# WHITTLE A WHIMMY DIDDLE

The easiest wood to carve is live or green wood that's young, light green, and sappy inside. Here's how to can make an Appalachian folk toy called a whimmy diddle and practice carving skills at the same time.

**You'll need:**

a sharp pocketknife

8-inch, 4-inch, and 2-inch sections of a green hardwood branch (oak, maple, beech)

a drill

1-inch nail

an adult helper

**1.**
Peel the bark from the hardwood pieces with the knife. Stroke the knife away from the body.

**2.**
The 8-inch piece will form the body. Whittle one end so it tapers to a point.

**3.**
Cut six evenly spaced notches along one side of the body. Each notch should be less than a quarter-inch.

**4.**
The four-inch piece will be the rubbing stick. Whittle half of it so it tapers to a point, too.

**5.**
The short piece becomes a propeller. Whittle the top and bottom until it is flat.

**6.**
Whittle into the center, front, and back, so that the piece looks like a pinched hourglass. It should be balanced so the thickness from the center to the top and to the bottom is about the same.

**7.**
Ask an adult to help drill a hole through the pinched center of the propeller and slip the nail through it.

**8.**
Cut off the very end of the body piece. Push the nail into the flat tip.

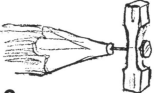

**9.**
Hold the opposite end of the body piece in one hand and rub up and down the notches with the rubbing stick in the other hand. The propeller should turn. If it doesn't, cut the notches deeper until the propeller does spin.

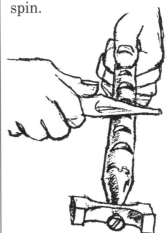

# WHITTLE A WHISTLE

**L**ick your lips, pucker, and blow. If nothing comes out, here's how to whittle a bark whistle and make plenty of noise.

| You'll need: |
| --- |
| a pocketknife |
| green willow, poplar, basswood, or other smooth-bark tree or shrub branch, 1/2 inch thick and 4 inches long |
| water |
| an adult helper |

### 1.

Slice through the bark, stopping at the wood, three-fourths inch from one end of the branch. Then wet your whistle in water for half an hour.

### 2.

Pound all over the wet bark with a closed pocketknife or stick. This will loosen the bark, but take care not to crack it.

### 3.

Hold the ends of the stick with both hands, twist, and pull the pounded bark off the stick in one piece. It should come off clean as a whistle. Once it's off, slip the bark tube back on again.

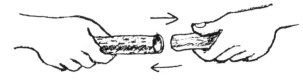

### 4.

To make the mouthpiece, cut a diagonal chunk from the end, through the stick and loose bark, as shown. Set it aside. Turn the whistle over and cut a notch, also through bark and wood, on the other side. Slip the stick out of the bark tube again.

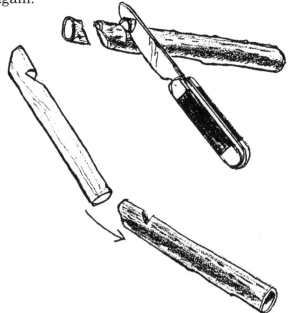

**5.**

Working with the bare stick, chop off the end at the notch. Slice a sliver from the top of this end piece to make an air passage and slip the stick in the bark tube.

**6.**

Trim the set-aside piece of stick flat to make a tight plug for the opposite end of the bark tube. Now blow the whistle.

## WHISTLE SUGGESTIONS

- Try making whistles of different lengths—longer whistles make lower notes.

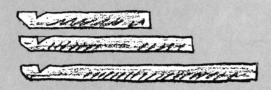

- For a whistle that'll make a whooping noise, don't plug the end. Instead, whittle a movable plunger, as shown, that can be slid back and forth in the tube to make different notes while blowing.

- For a one-note whistle that warbles, put a dried pea in the tube before plugging the end.

## WHISTLE SAYINGS

The sayings "wet your whistle" and "clean as a whistle" come from the age-old craft of making whistles from willow bark, as described here.

# KNOTS AND STITCHES

**M**any of these summer projects require special knots or stitches. Keep the hammock swinging and the flag flying by using some of these knots.

## THE ANATOMY OF ROPE

Get ready to tie knots by learning the parts of the rope and the basic moves used in tying.

**1.**

Rope has three parts: the working end, the standing part, and the bight.

The working end is the end that's tied.

The bight is a bend in the rope between the working end and the standing part.

The standing part is not tied but can be used in tightening the knot.

**2.**
There are two kinds of loops.

An overhand loop is formed by the working end crossing over the standing part.

An underhand loop is formed when the working end is passed under the standing part.

**3.**
An overhand knot is created when the working end is passed through an overhand loop and tightened.

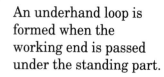

# THE HALF HITCH

The half hitch is the most secure knot for tying a boat to a dock or an anchor rope to a boat or a cleat. Make double half hitches and a boat will be truly safe.

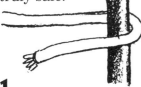

**1.**

Wrap the rope around a post on the dock or through a cleat.

**2.**

Pass the working end of the rope under the rope and loop it back over the rope attached to the boat.

**3.**

Pass the working end under the boat line again and loop back toward the post or cleat. Pull tight.

# THE LOOP KNOT

The loop knot is a variation of a slip knot. When used in making a swing, it secures the tire, leaving two pieces of rope free to attach the tire to a tree.

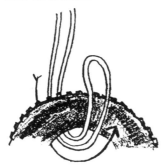

**1.**

Fold the rope in half. Pass the loop end through the tire.

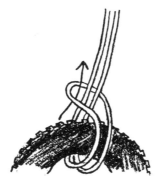

**2.**

Pass the two loose ends of rope through the loop and pull tight around the tire.

# CLOVE HITCH ON A POLE

This is a specialty knot for tying rope to a pole or post.

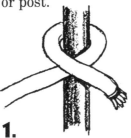

**1.**

Bring the working end of the rope across the front of the pole, around the back and over the standing part again, forming an X with the ropes.

**2.**

Wrap the working end around the back again and slide the end under the X in the front. Pull tight.

# CLOVE HITCH ON A TOGGLE

**1.**

Form two loops exactly as shown. The bottom loop has the rope going in front of the loop, and the top loop has the rope going toward the back.

**2.**

Overlap the two loops, slipping the bottom loop behind the top loop.

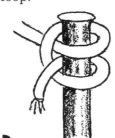

**3.**

Slip the overlapped loops over the toggle and pull to tighten.

MORE

# SHEET BEND

The sheet bend knot is used to join together two ropes of different thicknesses.

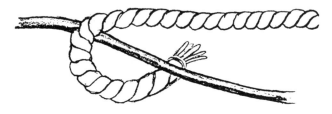

**1.**

Let the thinner rope hang or lie straight. Loop the thick rope around the thin rope.

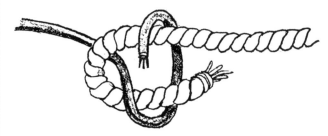

**2.**

Take the loose end of the thin rope and pass it under the end of the thick rope, up and over the top of the thick rope, back under the thin rope, and out through the loop formed by the thick rope.

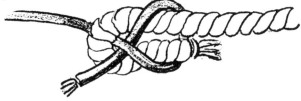

**3.**

Pull gently on the two loose thick ropes, and the loose end of the thin rope to tighten.

# THE SQUARE KNOT

The square knot is used to attach two ropes that are the same size or two ends of the same rope.

**1.**

Form a loop with each of the two ropes.

**2.**

Slip the left-hand loop through the right-hand loop.

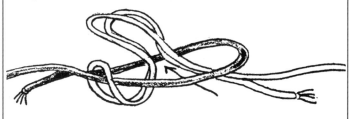

**3.**

Bring the loose ends of the right-hand loop through the left-hand loop.

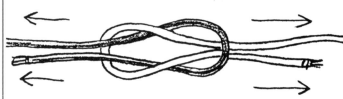

**4.**

Pull the loose ends out to tighten.

## **SO YOU CAN** SEW

Threading a needle is a simple but essential skill for any sewing job. Once it's learned, it's hard to forget.

**1.**

Choose a needle suitable to the task. If the cloth is heavy, such as denim, use a large, thick needle. For beading, use a very thin, long needle. Thread varies in thickness. Choose a thick thread for a large needle, and thin thread for a beading needle.

**2.**

Cut a piece of thread no longer than the length of an arm. It's better to use several pieces for a project than to have a long thread snarl into knots.

**3.**

Wet the end of the thread in the mouth and pinch it with your teeth to make it flat. Insert the thread through the eye of the needle, using a steady hand. It helps to have good light.

**4.**

Double the thread—pull it to equal lengths—or leave one end shorter than the other. Tie a knot at the end of a single thread or knot a double thread together to prevent the thread from pulling straight through the fabric when sewing.

## BLANKET STITCH

A blanket stitch is used to attach the soft binding to the end of an itchy wool blanket. It's an excellent stitch to use when finishing an edge.

**1.**

Thread the needle and make a knot. Pull the needle and thread through an outside edge of the fabric (or cardboard).

**2.**

Make the blanket stitches by bringing the needle under the edge to the bottom side, then poking it up through the fabric with the sharp end of the needle pointing toward the outside edge. Pull the needle through the loop. Pull gently to tighten.

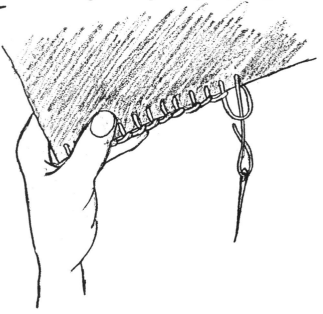

# INDEX